A Hut of One's Own

The MIT Press Cambridge, Massachusetts London, England

Ann Cline

A Hut of One's Own

Life Outside the Circle of Architecture

This book was set in Janson by Graphic Composition, Inc.

Printed and bound in the United States of America.

Library of Congress Cataloging-in-Publication Data

Cline, Ann.
    A hut of one's own : life outside the circle of architecture / Ann Cline.
        p.   cm.
    Includes bibliographical references and index.
    ISBN 0-262-53150-X (pbk.)
    1. Huts.   2. Dwellings—Psychological aspects.   3. Vernacular architecture—Psychological aspects.   I. Title.
    GT170.C55   1998
    392.3′6—dc21   97-33107
                                                                          CIP

Frontispiece: Floating Fall Tea, Chicago River, 1992

For Peter and Wayne and
in memory of my father and mother

Contents

Suppose that Architecture draws a circle around itself and proclaims—imperious Architecture!—that everything inside the circle *is* Architecture and that everything outside *is not*. From a great distance—from, say, a picnic bench set up in the middle of the Sea of Tranquillity—this circle appears to be a sharp, unambiguous demarcation; an impenetrable line of continuous length and no width. There is no mistaking what lies inside the circle, be it the Pazzi Chapel or Fallingwater, for what lies outside—the realm of bookkeepers, bumblebees, and subatomic particles.

As we approach more closely the line swells and blurs. What we have taken for a wall, inert and opaque, is now more accurately described as a zone several miles across, possessing a breathable atmosphere, and teeming with life.

In *A Hut of One's Own* we will take a stroll through these borderlands that surround Architecture—a region of structures and ideas, a wasteland of heterodoxy defined simultaneously by its proximity to Architecture and its proximity to everything else. On our way we will discover simple structures: shacks, teahouses, follies, *casitas*. Here and there, we will observe ritual practices dedicated to various "Gods," "Goods," or goods, and we will (over)hear the practitioners of construction, art, and biology discuss beauty, satisfaction, freedom, survival, and ethics.

Whenever we wander very near to what Architecture most certainly *is*, we will catch glimpses of shadowy figures slipping out—as if to a secluded dacha, where they have arranged a clandestine rendezvous with other partisans and malcontents, and then slipping back in again. These figures are the protagonists in our story.

Preface

This book, then, is about eccentrics and recluses, hut dwellers and ne'er-do-wells, a story about lives scribbled in the margins of architecture and history, of huts and follies that would be forgotten but for the curious way misanthropy occasionally turns beneficent.

More than only a story, this book is also an essay that attempts to overturn Architecture's victory over Individual Experience. Here we will look at dwellings that were not well attuned to the architecture of their era and at their builders, whose lives may instead have been ahead of their time, as if their very inability to march in step raised exactly those cultural issues that later on became helpful.

While this collection's limits will appear arbitrary, from my point of view all of the sights encountered on our stroll—the follies and tea huts, their rituals and antirituals (together with the ideas people have held about them)— have this in common: all acquired their significance during times of cultural transition, when one picture of the world overlapped with its successor. And it is this, in turn, which gives purpose and prejudice to our journey. Right now, comparable transitions are at work; right now, shadowy figures are moving from the circle of Architecture to rendezvous with primitive huts and their avant-gardes, with their makers and denizens.

I know, for I am one of them.

Opening Interval

The Hut in My Mind

In the courtyard of California's Tassajara Hot Springs, I met a contemporary hut dweller. It was his habit to drop into Tassajara from time to time, after tourist season had closed. Mike, as I will call him, exchanged his labor for meals and lodging. I was told that he had been among a group of patients requiring long-term psychiatric care who had been released from state institutions some years earlier.

Since smoking was only permitted in the courtyard, I often found Mike there hoping to bum a cigarette. Once I obliged him, I learned that he usually lived in the mountains near Santa Cruz in a hut he had built from scrap materials. Thereafter we often fell into conversations about such hut builders' topics as the plentiful supply of triangular plywood (left over from sheathing the gable end of pitched roof houses) and how to form columns or posts from two-by-four stubs. Aside from his being exceptionally soft-spoken, I could never detect Mike's psychological problem.

In fact, it delighted me to finally talk with someone who knew many of the same things I had discovered, and Mike was surprised that an architecture professor had any such interests. I told him that I too had built my own hut and lived in it for a year. At first I don't think he believed me, but I think he began to when I told him I thought that once a person had experienced life from inside a hut, he or she would never find any other life so satisfying.

"A hut," he said emphatically, "is the best place to live."

The biggest problem, he added, was bathing. He had tried coiling a length of dark garden hose on the roof to heat water, but as he said, "this only works when there's sun and it helps if the hose doesn't leak much." The second biggest problem, he said, was that people tried to persuade him to find "someplace else to live more *comfortable*"—a shelter was then generally recommended. "But my hut *is* comfortable," he pleaded a case I already accepted. "It's what I want."

Sitting in Tassajara's cold mountain stream at the spot the hot springs entered, I felt a shiver of pleasure I had not felt in a long time—the same shiver I had felt when I sat in the frame of my hut, just barely cocooned in an active world not of my making. As I watched the water tumble toward me, a silent scene but for an occasional jay echoing in the canyon, I recalled the mountain poems of Chinese and Japanese hut dwellers who had been my hut's comrades and the shivers I felt as I recognized their long past world in the very world around me.

I remembered the first time I'd had such a shiver, in a tiny lean-to shelter I had as a kid: a fierce storm had blown up suddenly and with rain drumming on the roof, I was unable to leave. Still, warm and dry inside, I imagined a more ambitious life in this hut than my young years could accomplish. I shivered with excitement at a prospect I could then not have even described, a prospect that had required adulthood to approach: the pleasure of a small dwelling intensely inhabited and occasionally shared—a hut of one's own.

When I got ready to leave Tassajara, Mike asked if I'd send a picture of my hut to a friend's address in Santa Cruz where he could pick up mail. He said he hoped I'd write the book I told him I was planning.

Finally he added, "If you tell people about *your* hut, then maybe they'll let me have *mine*."

What Mike didn't know, what I perhaps could not have explained to him, was that even architecture professors who espoused hut life invited hassles. Even though I had just earned tenure, I had done so by keeping my hut life buried, covered over with competition entries and modest commissions. But now, with tenure, I was free to be a hut builder, free to examine the place of hut dwelling in a professionally focused world.

In the ten years since I revealed my secret life to Mike, I revealed it to others as well—students, colleagues, strangers, and friends. But ironically, just as I was coming out as a hut builder, the subject of huts gradually appeared out in the world. Pavilions and follies, as icon or as bauble, spiced up projects from Louisville to Paris. People who knew about my interest in huts sent me articles and photos, but as the evidence accumulated, I realized these huts were not what I had in mind. They seemed to have no life going on inside them; they were objects, not experience.

I grew defensive trying to explain the difference until finally I wrote a story, a fiction-documentary, in which the huts I had in mind were presented as real: "These places exist in most American cities and suburbs, although they are often obscure and difficult to locate," I wrote with feigned authority.

I continued in the same quasi-reportorial style: "The practice of gathering in huts was begun primarily to address the time in the lives of the young when formal schooling ended and the responsibilities of contributive roles began. It was initially the young who sought out these huts, who first imagined them out of their deep need for life to be something more than role and rote, who could not—without these huts or a similar device—stare ahead to their lives without banality and boredom returning their glance. To them, the hut was a hopeful sign; a place and time set aside to continue the inquiry with which schooling teased them, like strippers do. For them, the hut became their own school, with its own rules. Conversations could begin slowly, or not at all; topics could mingle or remain on track; participants could float in and out. In some of the huts, bells actually rang on the hour and at ten minutes before, which, it delighted them, they were free to ignore."

Another constituency of these huts were young artists. "Brought up in a world of big names who monopolize the high-priced walls of gallery and museum—thereby limiting the supply of investible art and thereby also choosing those who could sustain their lives by their art—these huts were both studio and gallery. There the act of making and viewing, the roles of artist and audience, the aspects of product and production were one. The activities' focus mattered little. It may have been, on one occasion, that what happened there was merely the mixing of pigments—an act so full of unique life as to eclipse, often, whatever might be made of them. Those who viewed art as the accumulation of inspired artifacts saw neither progress nor investment in these hut artists. But precisely because the old system of patronage ignored them for so long, these artists were able to develop a rich, independent—and seemingly paradoxical—tradition of moment before anyone realized or exploited it for fame or fortune.

"Many of the early huts were created for tea making, or for coffee making, and many hut artists took training in these arts, although as many had at one time studied dance, martial arts, performance, mime, meditation, theater. Soon, however, there appeared huts with masters who told stories or who provoked poetry or discourse, who practiced magic or seance, who explored fable or fetish—who, in short, encapsulated the rich opportunity for moments of engagement brought about by existence as a human being. By these moments, increasing numbers of people saw as miraculous and whimsical the temporary forms of energy in the universe and engaged in an appreciation of them so long as life and breath held together body, mind, and spirit."[1]

A Hut of One's Own

Primitive Huts

one

Life in the Margins

Even though no modern Western culture encourages hut dwelling, still everyone knows what "the hut" stands for. Our literature and art abound with them. Hieronymus Bosch portrays St. Anthony in a hut, immobile in the face of worldly temptations. When Lady Chatterly and Mellors finally succumb to their "natural" desires, it happens inside the gamekeeper's hut. And when Johanna Spyri's Heidi is shipped off to her grandfather she goes to his hut, high up in the Alps.

Sweet, sacred, and profane, these stories pull the reader's imagination into the "hut dream," which Gaston Bachelard has called "the tap-root of inhabiting." In the hut, he tells us, "destitution gives access to absolute refuge."[1] Moreover, within these spare circumstances, nothing can be taken for granted.

Po-i and Shu-ch'i learned this the hard way. Remembered by ages to come from a poem they left behind, these two sages were the world's first recorded recluses. They retreated from the reign of Emperor Wu Wang, around 1000 B.C., to nearby mountains, living on "ferns and dew."

> Ascending West Mountain, we pick its wild ferns.
> He [Wu Wang] does not know that he is substituting tyranny
>   for tyranny.
> If the age of Shen-nung, Shun and Yu is gone forever,
> Where shall we betake ourselves.
> Alas, we depart this world;
> The times are hopelessly decadent.[2]

Curiously, knowing as he did that Po-i and Shu-ch'i eventually starved to death in their reclusion, in similarly troubled times half a millennium later the philosopher Lao Tzu would also recommend refuge: "Block all passages, shut the doors, and till the end your strength shall not fail. Open up the passages, increase your doings, and till your last day no help shall come to you. . . ."[3] Even so, Lao Tzu counseled neither martyrdom nor exile. Instead, he recommended distance. He invited the refuge seeker to imagine a life where, "though the neighboring settlement might be so near he could hear the cocks crowing and the dogs barking, he would grow old and die without ever having been there." In this place, Lao Tzu suggested, the recluse might live "contented with his food, pleased with his clothing, satisfied with his home, taking pleasure in his rustic tasks."[4]

The pleasure Lao Tzu holds out as the outcome of reclusion (which is not incidental to our story as it will evolve) takes the place of more socially contingent rewards: power, success, wealth—precisely those pursuits Lao Tzu finds risky in unsettled times. Of course, for those without social aspirations, Lao Tzu merely describes ordinary life. The pursuit of ordinariness is interesting culturally when extraordinary people do it, when educated people find satisfaction in domiciles like those of hoi polloi, a satisfaction more commonly sought than we might imagine.

What began after Lao Tzu as a trickle of gentlemen recluses had, a thousand years later, turned into a steady stream. Educated cosmopolites retired to the mountains and there recorded their lives in verse and in painting. The latter formed a major genre that illustrates the recluse poet's world: most typically a tiny hut set in some particularly interesting aspect of a vast mountain terrain crisscrossed by narrow paths, along which one or two human figures amble, gazing out at the vista. This recluse living apart from the world, aware of it (and later, it aware of him) but participating only in his immediate world, would eventually extend his influence not only back to the cities he abandoned, but to distant shores—Japanese and European.

Parallel to these stories are two others, half a world away. Like the recluse poets of China, the Greek philosopher Heraclitus lived in remote and modest circumstances. As legend has it, one day some important visitors came looking for him. They found an old man inside a hut, bent over a cooking fire. Assuming he was a servant, they asked to see the great philosopher. When the old man identified himself as the person they sought, the visitors exclaimed, "But, what are you doing *here*?"

Gesturing to his humble surroundings, Heraclitus replied, "Even here, the gods reside."

Conversely, we recall not just one hut dweller in the early Christian world but many—the fourth-century "desert fathers." Isolated from their cities, in "cells" that cannot have been much different from Heraclitus's hut, these recluses sought, in Thomas Merton's words, "their own true self, in Christ." In method, their search was not unlike Lao Tzu's; they rejected the false, formal self, "fabricated under social compulsion in 'the world'. . . [and] sought a way to God that was uncharted and freely chosen, not inherited from others who had mapped it out beforehand."[5] As with the hut-dwelling poets of China, we can recall the desert fathers now because some of their writing survived. These two groups differed, however, in fundamental ways.

While the recluse poets followed Lao Tzu's lead and took pleasure in their rustic surroundings, the desert fathers did battle with that pleasure. The abbot Mark, noting that it is "good to have nothing in your cell that gives you pleasure," tells of another who found a wildflower growing in his cell. He pulled it out by its roots. To this, the abbot Arsenius remarked that, even though this action was all right and each man should follow his own spiritual way, if a brother were "not able to get along without the flower, he should plant it again."[6]

By contrast, the recluse poet revels in his ordinary existence and, indeed, in every plant around him:

> The weather changeable at dusk and dawn,
> mountain waters shot through with clear light,
> a clear light that makes men joyful;
> the wanderer, lulled, forgets to go home.
> Out of the valley, the sun still high;
> boarding the boat, the light fading now,
> forest and ravine clothed in sombering color,

clouds of sunset wrapped in evening mist;
lotus and caltrop, their leaves one by one shining;
reeds and cattails propped against each other—
push through, hurry down the trail to the south,
returning contented to bed behind the eastern door.
Thoughts at ease, outside things weigh lightly;
mind relaxed, nothing going wrong.
A word to you gentlemen "nourishers of life"
try using this method for a while![7]

From the recluse poet's viewpoint, the Christian ascetic's position seems curious. On the one hand, each man should find his own way; even so, the pleasure of the wildflower is all right for the Christian ascetic only if he can't get along without it—presumably a weakness. Such tests of strength not only seem remote but would have been absurd for the Taoist. Still, in the West, this pathetic battle between the wildflower and human will draws a line in the sand between simple pleasures and spiritual good, a line later extended to keep rustic tasks and places in a marginal position in relation to, first, an abstracted God and, later, even abstraction itself.

When we find Sir Christopher Wren comparing customary beauty (the love of the mutable and arbitrary beauty found in things begotten by use and familiarity) with natural beauty (despite its name, the love of simple, abstract geometrical—therefore, eternal and "natural"—forms), we see the line drawn in the sand has shifted very little; it has only been extended to another time and place.

Even now, the word *pleasure* prompts a quickening and a confusion. Roland Barthes points out that no word simultaneously covers the pleasure of contentment and the pleasure of bliss or rapture: "Therefore, 'pleasure' here (and without our being able to anticipate) sometimes extends to bliss, sometimes is opposed to it."[8] The pleasure of the text, the pleasure of the rustic's hut: sometimes there is bliss, sometimes contentment, and the two pleasures are as opposed as the beauties of custom and geometry.

I wonder if the quickening and the confusion aroused by our own shanty-dwelling recluses—the urban homeless who dwell in our midst—result from our having extended that same line drawn in the sand to our time, dividing the hut dwellers of serene contentment from the hut dwellers of misanthropic bliss.

In either case, our view rests on the hut dwellers' attitude. Without knowing their intentions, we tend to view them all as simply "poverty-stricken" persons, their huts as mere hovels. Even so, James Agee equivocally points out the beauty of such abodes:

> It seems to me necessary to insist that the beauty of [this sharecropper's] house, inextricably shaped as it is in an economic and human abomination, is at least as important a part of the fact as the abomination itself: but that one is qualified to insist on this only in proportion as one faces the brunt of his own "sin" in so doing. . . . But . . . the "sin" in my present opinion is in feeling the least apologetic for perceiving the beauty of [these] houses.[9]

Habitations

The Chinese recluse poets might well have felt at home in the primitive hut of Heraclitus, and the desert fathers would no doubt have cherished the notion of "living on ferns and dew," yet each group withdrew for different reasons. Nevertheless, as the Oriental and Occidental recluse drew closer to the collective life of culture, or of cities, these sharp differences in purpose diminished. When reclusion took on a social dimension, it became soft. It lost the edge that had come first from the uncertainty of physical survival and later from the condition of tabula rasa that reclusion had afforded. Here every condition and thought could be considered and reconsidered, literally from the ground up.

In China, the educated class, barred from farming, business, or crafts, had only two courses open: civil service or retirement. The latter, as it became popular, degenerated toward affectation; "recluse poets" retired to the mountains, often with vast retinues or as a ploy, to feign disinterest in outcomes they still hoped to affect.

The recluse poet's influence extended back to the cities
A Summer Pavilion with Pines, Hsü Shin-chang

A mutable and arbitrary beauty begotten by use and familiarity
Mississippi River cottage near La Crosse, Wisconsin, c. 1920

The ornamental hermit became a surrogate for gentlemanly escape
Sanctuary of the Hermit Finch at Burley-on-the-Hill, Leicestershire

Nameless hut dwellers on the margins of cities today
Islais Creek Channel, San Francisco, 1988

9 *Habitations*

During the T'ang dynasty (c. 600–900), recluse poets and painters gained an audience among those who did not actively seek retirement. Paradoxically, the recluse poet became famous. As city dwellers eagerly sought his poems and paintings, the Chinese mountain hut dweller became a phenomenon. By the late T'ang and into the Sung dynasty (c. 900–1300), the mode of official life changed as well. The desire for seclusion, or *yin*, literally "concealment," (not unlike Bachelard's "refuge") found an urban form, *shin-yin*, literally "retirement in the city." Now the Chinese civil servant might create a wilderness landscape within the gates and fences of his town dwelling.

The treatise on gardening, *Yüan-Yeh*, tells us that in a well-planned garden one may live as a hermit right in the middle of town:

> A single "mountain" may give rise to many effects, a small stone may evoke many feelings. The shadow from the dry leaves of the banana tree is beautifully outlined on the paper of the window. The roots of the pine force their way through the crevices of the hollow stones . . . If one can find stillness in the midst of the city turmoil, why should one then forego such an easily accessible spot and seek a more distant one?[10]

A typical Chinese gentleman kept at least some portion of his walled-in garden as wilderness and while he went into the streets as a civil servant by day, at night he returned to become a mountain recluse. The poet Po Chu-i (c. 800) writes, then, not of a rural but of an urban seclusion:

> I am not suited for service in a country town;
> At my closed door autumn grasses grow.
> What could I do to ease a rustic heart?
> I planted bamboos, more than a hundred shoots.
> When I see their beauty, as they grow by the stream-side,
> I feel again as though I lived in the hills,
> And many a time when I have not much work

Round their railing I walk till night comes.
Do not say their roots are still weak;
Do not say their shade is still small;
Already I feel that both in the courtyard and house
Day by day a fresher air moves.
But most of all I love, lying near the window-side,
To hear in their branches the sound of the autumn
      wind.[11]

So, while only poets and painters explored reclusion during the T'ang dynasty, their vision more widely flourished under the Sung dynasty. Re-creating rustic landscapes in the very cities from which the recluse poets had departed, while tempering the extreme position and rusticity of the recluse, tempered the urbanity of the city dweller as well. If, in his nonworking hours, the civil servant duplicated activities of the distant recluse—"lying near the window-side"—what other activities did he displace? What lavish banquets and spectacles did he forego? Certainly not all. However, now the sophisticated cosmopolite likely possessed as well the complete rustic package: the recluse's garden, his poetry and painting, and eventually also his beverage of choice, tea.

When the Japanese imported the Sung-dynasty recluse package, they could place themselves and their own literary recluses—like Kamo no Chomei and Yoshida Kenko—within this new vision. The Japanese tea ritual, then, grew from this syncretism between native sensibility and Chinese Sung culture. What seems like a mere social occasion—and was so for the Chinese gentleman—became a precise and exacting ritual of landscape inhabitation, where the Japanese teahouse actualized the Chinese recluse painter's abode.

Not so easily reconciled with Sung sensibilities was seventeenth-century European culture. First of all, Western traders only made substantial connection with China after the Sung dynasty's demise. Moreover, the imported artifact of choice was neither poetry nor painting but porcelain, a technical advance in ceramics previously unknown in the West. A little like a Coca-Cola bottle dropping from an airplane into an aboriginal tribe—as in *The Gods Must Be Crazy*—Europeans received porcelain with amazement. The culture that produced it quickly became the object of imaginative speculation. Many porcelain imports had small snippets of poetry painted on them, which the Japanese could translate, but the Europeans generally could not. Instead, the Europeans more readily understood the images of huts and mountain landscapes that also frequently decorated these treasures. Once Europeans themselves mastered the art of porcelain making, their mimicry of Chinese scenes gave way to depictions of their own landscape. Meanwhile, however, the allure of these strange mountain huts with their craggy settings and equally craggy inhabitants fired another kind of imitation, something like—but in other ways altogether different from—the Japanese mimicry found in the tea ritual.

The poet Dame Edith Sitwell recounts one of the most bizarre aspects of this innocent influence in the practice of certain eighteenth-century gentlemen, who, "[t]rying to escape the consequences of being alive," installed ornamental hermits on their estates. "Nothing, it was felt, could give such delight to the eye, as the spectacle of an aged person with a long grey beard, and a goatish rough robe, doddering about amongst the discomforts and pleasures of Nature."[12] Dwelling in huts, which in one case provided a Bible, optical glasses, a mat, a hassock, and an hourglass, these ornamental hermits periodically received water and food from the main house. To assure the effect of their hermitage, the hermits signed contracts in which they promised not to cut hair, beard, or fingernails, and either to remain unseen or to be on display, to the gentleman and his friends. In this way, these hermits became surrogates for gentlemanly escape.

Had Europeans access to poetry recording the lives of the images they beheld, surrogate hermitage might not have sufficed. Behaving as if the secrets of this mysterious porcelain culture lay in imagery, not experience, they understood reclusion as a visual artifact. Even so, these images remained remote—a minor story within the passing fancy of chinoiserie. Besides, other primitive huts had already been discussed, closer to home—such as the one conjured by the Abbé Laugier.

The curious contrast between the ornamental hermit on exhibition and the recluse poet "taking pleasure in his rustic tasks," between the primitive hut as *image* and as *experience*, will come up again, in both the European folly and the Japanese tea ritual. For the moment, however, the significance of the desert fathers' and the recluse poets' anarchism is the position they established for themselves (and later, for others), distant from prevailing rules and conventional values. By taking this position, they did not necessarily place themselves above society as superior beings. Rather, their intention was to avoid the world where "men were divided into those who were successful, and imposed their will on others, and those who had to give in and be imposed upon."[13] In short, their reclusion took them away from concerns over success—and failure: Incipient Rousseau.

The subsequent project, bringing the experience of lives unfettered by convention closer to urban experience, required, in both the East and the West, the unwieldy and apparently ironic turn toward ritual. Unlike the rituals of religious life, the rituals of the primitive-hut-gone-urban (promulgated not only by Chinese gentlemen influenced by mountain poets, but by their Japanese imitators as well) eschewed symbolic meaning or dogmatic intention. Instead, these hut rituals share a somewhat different intention. Whether the disembodied eye of madness we will find in the Western folly and, later, in the art gallery, or the reembodied eye of meditation we will find in the Japanese teahouse, the ritual intention of all these primitive huts begins in physiology and existential philosophy, not in theology or dogma. The distance sought by the actual wilderness recluse is regained by his or her urban counterpart in a careful theatricality of place and performance. In this way, these urban rituals of primitive-hut inhabitation reclaimed some of reclusion's edge—its advantage—over more casual approaches.

In the process, these rituals buried the opportunity for unconventional experiences inside convention itself. The power of these rituals to disrupt, enrich, unite, or divide their host cultures actually ties together experiences we generally hold apart; what we usually view as culturally unique may hold some promise for cultural syncretism as well.

To return to the margins of our own cities today and the nameless hut dwellers in our midst, I am aware—despite the Eastern and Western examples I have just glossed over—that there may be some who will resist any effort to position a homeless person's shack in relationship to these more ideal primitive huts. Perhaps my own impulse to so position the shack dweller comes from a childhood memory.

Near a cottage where we lived every summer, a one-room hut built of mismatched cinder block sat far back from the road. A large vegetable garden surrounded the structure and, from time to time, I saw a weathered old man tending his vegetables or beginning his ride into town on an old bicycle. When I was old enough to be curious, I asked adults who this person was. "That's Crazy Ben," they said.

"Why is he crazy?" I must have asked. I only remember something about a failed romance a long time ago, and a choice thereafter to live in a hut he had made with his own hands. I must have been a dim child: I could never figure out what was so crazy about Ben and, even now, I still can't.

Nor would I be surprised to learn that Thoreau's neighbors called him Crazy Henry.

What might contribute to the difference is that one wrote and published, and the other did not; one ate Sunday dinner at the Emerson table, and the other lacked a patron. Still, it seems likely that what was at stake for both of them is not all that different. And, it seems to me, now, that what was at stake for Ben was not unlike what was at stake for the desert fathers, or for the Chinese mountain recluses either. In troubled times, they all sought to experience life away from social definitions of success or failure. From there, these primitive huts marked personal, original inquiries into the ever mysterious nature of human existence.

In a profound sense, these primitive huts amount to much the same thing and that thing is not unimportant—even now.

What Is Really at Stake

The attempt to acquire reclusion's grace by sponsoring an ornamental hermit might strike us as eccentric, yet the Abbé Laugier's approach to the primitive hut was nearly as odd.

Not a hut dweller himself, Marc-Antoine Laugier— Louis XV's outspoken Jesuit preacher turned Benedictine Abbé and *homme de belles-lettres* —gained fame for his *Essai sur L'architecture*. In this work, Laugier's business with the primitive hut—"the first hut made by man"—was purely speculative. He needed to establish a "primitive hut" because his theory of architecture would derive its logic and authenticity from the hut's originating principles—principles so basic that, as he would argue, all further architecture should be derived from them. But, lacking any evidence of a primitive hut, Laugier was undaunted; he made one up:

> Some branches broken off in the forest are material to his purpose. He chooses four of the strongest, and raises them perpendicularly to the ground, to form a square. On these four he supports four others laid across them; above these he lays some which incline to both sides, and come to a point in the middle. This kind of roof is covered with leaves thick enough to keep out both sun and rain: and now man is lodged.[14]

The abbot-philosophe believed that because it lacked the *universal* principles necessary for cultural coherence, architecture faced a crisis. In the primitive hut Laugier found his key principle: "a pure distillation of nature through unadulterated reason, prompted only by necessity."[15] In other words, the first primitive hut was *rational*.

Here Laugier saw himself continuing the great harvest of universal, timeless Truth from the tree planted earlier by Descartes. Having picked the lower branches clean of the fruits of certainty—like physics and astronomy—rationalists of Laugier's day now reached higher up in the tree, to the arts and to architecture.

At stake for Laugier and his cohorts, even beyond rationalism, was abstract and theoretical thinking. Unlike the actual huts of Heraclitus or the desert fathers, the Enlightenment's primitive hut existed in theory, not experience. Not even the ornamental hermit's experience aroused sufficient interest to prompt his patron's actual participation. The life of the ornamental hermit became as much an object of detached, abstract speculation as was Laugier's primitive man. Only the folly, eventually, will attempt not only construction but habitation as well.

How different, then, to find in Japan Kamo no Chomei's (c. 1200) hut fulfilling not a *theoretical* but an *existential* purpose.

> Now that I have reached the age of sixty, and my life seems about to evaporate like the dew, I have fashioned a lodging for the last leaves of my years. It is a hut where, perhaps, a traveler might spend a single night; it is like the cocoon spun by an aged silkworm. . . . It is a bare ten feet square and less than seven feet high. . . . I have added a lean-to on the south and a porch of bamboo. On the west I have built a shelf for holy water, and inside the hut, along the west wall, I have installed an image of Amida (Buddha). . . . When, as chance has had it, news has come to me from the capital, I have learned how many of the great and mighty have died since I withdrew to this mountain. . . . Only in a hut built for the moment can one live without fears."[16]

The catastrophes that devastated Kyoto and all Japan toward the end of the Heian period (782–1185), an unfortunate confluence of warfare, famine, earthquake, and disease, most certainly caused some of the deaths to which Kamo no Chomei refers. Even so, survival—the goal of Lao Tzu's impulse toward reclusion—was not at stake for Kamo no Chomei. Kamo no Chomei was, after all, an old man; in a time of catastrophe, he probably sought less a prolongation than a peaceful termination for his life. If Laugier had been a theoretician, concerned with architectural principles, then Lao Tzu and Kamo no Chomei were both men of practice, concerned with the nature of human existence.

Catastrophe, though actually around the corner, was far from Laugier's concern. The Hundred Years' War was long past—the war that had precipitated the rationalists' "quest for certainty" in the first place, the quest to find universal principles apart from theological ones, principles upon which all factions might agree.[17] In Laugier's time, the momentum of the rationalists' quest continued and only expanding its scope seemed to be at stake.

Arguably, while the French Revolution and the Napoleonic Wars scattered and confused the rationalists, only the two world wars of this century halted their momentum. With these wars, practical hut dwellers reemerged. At first, like Lao Tzu, some sought survival in troubled times, but later some others, like Kamo no Chomei, sought existential closure.

About the time I first saw Crazy Ben, I also saw an amazing photograph in *Life* magazine. In a bombed-out city, a stair tower had survived. Isolated above the rubble, the stairs still stood intact. On them, a group of survivors had made a shelter by spanning from part of the stair's tread to some opposing and parallel ledge. Here life continued on a series of broad, ascending shelves. What few possessions remained—a cup, a plate, a tin canister, a candlestick—rested on intervening steps. What had been either valueless or precious before the bombs struck had become—now, in this dire circumstance, and irrespective of its former place or category—sacred to survival itself.

Later, I would muse more generally about life in the ruins when I encountered Piranesi's eighteenth-century drawings of hut dwellers who had set up shelters among the ruins of Rome. Like Agee's impoverished sharecroppers, these and untold others lived a mere and bare existence at the edge of survival. Agee has called these conditions "the classicisms of economic need." But there exists another, related classicism that appeals to those not facing immediate death but aware, all the same, of mortality: the classicism of *existential*

Hut dwellers set up shelters among the ruins of Rome
The Fontana dell'Acqua Giulia, Vedute di Roma series, G. B. Piranesi

A geese-viewing hut poised on a mechanism that rotates
Habitat, Pierre Bourgault, 1970

The cups, and so forth, aren't sacred; they belong to poetry
Interior, Habitat, Pierre Bourgault, 1970

A tribute to the longing engendered by absence
Puerto Rican *casita*, the Bronx, 1990

need. What is at stake here lies concealed in appearances—unknowable, yet measurable because humankind is mortal. What is at stake here is the *measure* of life.

Along a marsh in Canada, through which geese migrate each fall and spring, a hut sits poised on a mechanism by which its owner can rotate his or her view. The hut forms a perfect cube: sliding glass doors form two ends while the other two are solid, although one has cut into it separate spaces that perfectly hold two white cups, two plates, and brackets that hold two forks, two spoons, and so forth. These niches do not suggest the sacred, as they might were survival at stake. While the steps of the survivalist stair-tower abode were sufficient for the sacred mission of the necessary utensils they held, the cavities of the geese-viewing hut in Canada made the utensils they held precious. They do not feign survival, for that is not the issue. Instead, these utensils belong to poetry.

It shouldn't surprise us that existentialism arose out of the ashes of war. Whether existence was physically intimate with both earth and sky (as it was for those who found shelter in the ruined stair) or metaphorically so (for those deprived of loved ones), mere existence claimed the existentialist's interest. In the face of war's experience, speculation and theory paled. After war's end, mere existence was source enough of truth, cause enough for joy.

And so, while modernism may have appeared the same just before as after, the war tinged it with a joy in things the next generation found joyless, sterile, and cold. This next generation had no measure of the invisible joy of mere existence; they took such joy for granted. Today, those who would be existentialists find their joy less in the *universality* of existence than in the *specificity* of "regional realisms," like those espoused by Kenneth Frampton or Michael Benedikt.

At stake for these existentialists, as for Laugier, is an architecture seen to be in crisis. They, like Laugier, seek an answer in universal principles, but in this case the principles of history, memory, location, and region. It is therefore curious that these regionalists would end the crisis of modernism's universality with yet another universal premise. But while the modernist classicism assumes that everywhere the earth and sky are the same, the existentialist/regionalist argues that they are everywhere different; what is universal is that everywhere, there is earth and sky.

Meanwhile, for some, the classicism of economic need remains. To those who dwell "between hurt but invincible nature and the plainest cruelties and needs of human existence," there is no theoretical dilemma. The poor uncover *empirically* what architectural existentialists recover *theoretically*. And what is most at stake in each case is not found but *made* in the primitive hut.

Landscapes Recalled

Just beyond the historic center of San Juan, a shantytown of colorful *casitas* clings to a seaside slope, occasionally tempting the tourist's hungry camera.

Though they are bursting with independent initiative and democratic impulse, such shantytowns, from São Paolo to Ankara, embarrass modern social and physical planners. These shanties offend modern demands for safety and cleanliness. In their place most planners will picture high-rise apartments, all in a row.

But what if the planners' dreams come true, and the Puerto Rican shanty dwellers move to the apartments of modernity's meccas? What do they do there? They build *casitas*, that's what.

On "vacant" land in the Bronx, between apartment buildings and amid urban blight, former residents of San Juan construct little houses from "home," painting them bright colors. Some *casitas* have signs such as "Villa Puerto Rico," as if there might be some mistake. On summer nights, neighbors from the apartments sit around or inside the *casitas*, enjoying the night air and the camaraderie. At Christmas, there are pig roasts. At other seasons, other events.

Modern apartment living brings many benefits, of course, yet these benefits do not support the memory of home. However meager San Juan's shantytown is materially, the extreme trouble it takes to construct a *casita* in the Bronx and defend it—from authorities and from deadbeats—testifies to the longing engendered by absence.

What materialists would have us measure in poverty, poets would have us measure in longing. In this sense, and despite obvious, vast differences, the *casitas* of New York are an analog to Marie Antoinette's *hameau*.

But Marie's longing was greater than could be satisfied in a single dwelling. The spell of Rousseau's Romantic and speculative idealism drew her into longing for a "simple life" she had only peripherally experienced herself. More's the pity, since longing for one's own past fills out even minimal form with the details of memory. Marie's longing for the peasant life, however, needed all the accoutrements, all the details filled in. Surrounding a cottage for the queen, there had to be a water mill, a barn, a dovecote, and a dairy with a real herd of cows and a bevy of milkmaids; there had to be dwellings for the gardeners, fields tilled by real peasants, and flocks of perfumed sheep—eventually an entire village of the simple life, a *hameau*. Fatally, the queen of France had the means to make her own rurified Disneyland. So taken by the charade in which she starred day after day, she neglected her duties—and more disastrously—her court. At her end, no one came to befriend poor Marie but her companion in simplicity, a favored lady-in-waiting who had her own thatched cottage at Rambouillet, the Princess de Lamballe.

Such shenanigans may have outraged Rousseau's truly simple folk who failed to see solidarity in these gestures, but even more enraged were the high and middle bourgioisie. They could or would not stop the mob that tore Lamballe's heart from her body even before it parted Marie Antoinette from her own head.

The Japanese shogun Yoshimasa Ashikaga (c. 1480) had a more sensible longing. Like his cohorts, he was smitten with the Sung dynasty package: the paintings of recluse poets, the mountain-inspired gardens, the delicate mysteries of powdered green tea whipped up in an evocative bowl. This Sung Chinese package was delivered not by Rousseauian philosophers whose simple life was speculation, but by Zen Buddhist abbots who lived the simple life one day at a time.

As a sect, this brand of monasticism had already faced its own brush with outrage. In his edict announcing the demolition of 4,600 Buddhist temples and the return of 26,500 monks and nuns to lay life, the tenth-century Chinese emperor Wu Tsung stated, "If even one man fails to work the fields, someone must go hungry."

Even so, the Zen sect fared better than others. Wu Tsung found it difficult to flaunt his edict with a group that lived by the motto "a day without work—a day without eating," a group that found favor with Confucianists for their reliance on action over words, a group that had been invited into syncretic relationship with Taoists, who wore their poverty without bravado, and who avoided the insult of sanctimoniousness. A group such as this would scarcely have inspired outrage even among the Third Estate or the Paris Commune.

Yoshimasa really liked these guys; he longed to join them. In the foothills east of Kyoto, he built a tiny temple and later a small abbot's residence. Then he surrounded them both with a garden that looked exactly like nature— especially if you had only Chinese ink paintings to tell you what nature was.

Like Marie Antoinette, Yoshimasa Ashikaga ventilated his longing in a constructed tableau. But unlike Marie, Yoshimasa's tableau was no hideaway; he made it the political and cultural center of his regime. What further longing Yoshimasa had—to enter the paintings that inspired him to reclusion—he fulfilled through a man named Murata Shuko. At Yoshimasa's order, Shuko built a rustic hut near the center of the capital and, there, devoted himself to the art of cooking a meal and eating it, the art of infusing tea and drinking it.

Today, the remnants of Marie Antoinette's *hameau* still stand near the Petite Trianon and Yoshimasa's hermitage still

Longing for the peasant life needed all the accoutrements
The Hamlet, near the Petit Trianon, c. 1790

Yoshimasa's tableau was no hideaway
Yoshimasa Ashikaga's Togudo, Ginkakuji, Kyoto, c. 1490

Today the remnants of Marie Antoinette's **hameau** *still stand*
One of the hamlet's nine thatched cottages

Nothing remains of Shuko's hermitage but the legacy of Tea
Thatched teahouse, National Household Museum, Nara

stands on the grounds of the Silver Pavilion. However, nothing remains of Shuko's hermitage but the rich legacy of his rustic domesticity, retained in the Japanese tea ceremony, which traces its origins, in part, back to Shuko's hut and indirectly to Yoshimasa's longing. Even today, Tea fulfills the longing of many—for rustic simplicity, for a tiny hut, for a *casita* of memory, for a landscape recalled or maybe just imagined.

In our own time, we have additional ways to assuage our longing beside actual landscapes of brick and stone, plaster and thatch. For millions, music creates the landscape of longing. Blind Lemon Jefferson—"one guy alone, with a guitar and no options but to sing to ease his pain"—evokes a landscape reaching from the Mississippi Delta to Chicago to Newcastle, a landscape of rock-bottom necessity and passion, a landscape sucked by hunger into even the *hameaux* of suburbia.

Today, the black man's blues and the white man's rock and roll create invisible landscapes that leave no trace but the headphone cord—a landscape of imagined fulfillment that replaces the agony of possibility. Lives undefined by necessity but torn by choice find, in music, a landscape of existential authenticity and bottom-line passion. Two minutes of Ry Cooder's guitar creates an empty, dusty highway taking us to Paris, Texas, no matter where we hear it, no matter— or because—we haven't been there ourselves. The highway to Wim Wenders's haunting, yet ever-so-familiar *Paris, Texas*, is the road of modern longing: to be on some roads, but not all roads. The pain we feel comes less from the choices we make than from those we cannot consummate, those we leave behind. Longing knows no privilege.

Interval

The Hut in the Backyard

Then I built a hut of my own.

I liked the idea of a hut as a refuge, whether it was in the middle of a city or on a mountaintop, and so, the huts of Shuko and Kamo no Chomei inspired me the most. Survival wasn't the issue, of course, but retirement was. Young as I might have been, I wanted retirement and right away—not the permanent, gold-watch-and-pension retirement but the contentment of an evening's or a weekend's reclusion. Like a Chinese civil servant, I could imagine living part of my life in my backyard.

As happens often in my life, the right book came my way just when I needed it: Kakuzo Okakura's *The Book of Tea*. Okakura's description of a tea hut—"an ephemeral structure built to house a poetic impulse . . . devoid of ornamentation except what may be placed in it to satisfy some aesthetic need of the moment . . . purposely leaving some thing unfinished for the play of the imagination to complete"[18]—not only defined the hut I wanted to build but also outlined the vision I couldn't describe when, as a child, a storm caught me inside my lean-to hut. Okakura proposed a vast game of objects in a small space, a space separated from weather and season by the merest membrane: a small dwelling intensely inhabited and occasionally shared. I imagined an American tea ceremony.

Still, even armed with Okakura's poetic blueprints, when I contemplated building my first hut outdoors directly on site, I found the prospect scary. I had no prior experience of diminutive spaces save those formed in childhood: a discarded appliance box, with holes cut for door and windows; a sheet thrown over a card table; the underside of large shrubs pruned into halls and rooms; and, of course, the scraps of wood that had created my lean-to shelter. In a child's mind, these places inspire imagination and enchantment; they prompt a larger vision. Then we grow up. Diminutive space now becomes the backseat, then the frontseat of a car, or maybe the cabin of a train or a ship. We find such spaces tolerable, or even enchanting, because they can go places. They move.

To begin I built a simple platform—six feet by eight feet—with four corner columns supporting a pitched roof. Sitting on the platform's floor was like being in a gazebo; it had shade, breeze, and view. But as with all gazebos, sitting there also exposed me to prying eyes. This was not a refuge yet.

As the autumn rains came, the idea of enclosure turned immediate. But quickly nailing plywood and cardboard temporarily to the frame put me back inside the appliance box again, scale for scale, as if I were a child but one who'd outgrown her imagination. Of the crude openings I left in these thoughtless walls, those nearest the floor brought me the most pleasure: by extending the floor to the surrounding ground, nearby tree trunks and falling leaves, unremarkable in full view, became passionate vignettes.

Still, the wind howled through these openings. This would be an asset in summer, although, for now, windows would help. But windows of what sort?

A single pane of glass stopped the wind but also rendered inconsequential the objects I'd brought there—a couple of books, a few bowls, an old kettle. Next to such yawning openings, these objects had no presence. Although my training told me no, my instincts suggested that old-fashioned mullioned windows might be the answer. But this was the 1960s; fashion had not yet turned "postmodern." Then, you couldn't buy a mullioned window anywhere but at a scrap yard. There window sash came in all sizes and shapes of once-were houses awaiting the homeowner who'd discovered dry rot or termites, who'd come for a close approximation.

Despite the plentiful supply, most scrap-yard window sash proved too large for my hut. In relationship to the kettle, for example, or to the person sitting beside it, these windows were out of scale. I bought only the smallest, and as they gradually found a place in my hut's temporary walls, I cut plywood panels to fit around them.

One day I found the smallest window of all—about eighteen inches square with four unbroken panes of glass. It rested, not with the others but flat, beneath one end of a steel I-beam. I persuaded the yard chief that any other piece of wood would as well keep the beam from rusting, but only because I had become a habitué could I also persuade him to call the yard crew together—to hoist the beam a few inches as I extracted my prize and slipped a block of wood in its place. Later, when I placed the square window among the others, it was like adding the last piece to a puzzle. After that, the kettle, the books, and the bowls were finally at rest.

Sitting inside felt a little like entering a Vermeer painting—but even more compressed—as if Vermeer's table had been pushed up against the windows with the walls drawn in around the table's edge. On top of the table—really the hut's floor—I could sit next to "Vermeer's kettle," next to his window. From there I could watch the rain collect and drip from the eave, taking part in a still life of objects and a not-so-still nature.

The hut's first challenge, then, involved scale: the scale of objects and persons in relationship to openings and enclosure. Abstractly conceived, scale is a tricky business. The tea men before me knew this, and so designed and built their huts as a process of trial, error, and rebuilding until the result *felt* firm, at rest, grounded in space. Firmness of structure or of sufficient stoutness turns out to be no trick at all when compared with the *impression* of firmness that results only from scale.

Having built my hut, I now faced the challenge of using it—not just now and then but almost daily, as Heraclitus, Shuko, Komo no Chomei, and the desert fathers had done: to sleep, to eat, to read. Where in all the emptiness of space was each to occur? As Carlos Castañeda had circled Don Juan's porch to find his own *sitio*, so I circled my hut looking for the tasks of my daily life. Where should I enter? Where would I sit? Where could I lie down?

The first entrance I made prompted me to build a tiny porch roof, supported by a slim piece of tree trunk. But after

Tree trunks and falling leaves became passionate vignettes

The square window where kettle and bowl were finally at rest

I frequently found myself sitting at the doorway, scribbling in my notebook, I filled the opening with a window, and below it a small writing shelf. While I no longer had an entrance, I did have a place for my books. One day as I lay on my side, I looked out to where a double-hung window rested vertically against the fence. I had always thought the window, a neighbor's donation, too large to be usable. But when I viewed it sideways, I saw a low, glass door sliding open horizontally—one you had to crawl into, the equivalent of my hut's *nijiri-guchi*, or "wriggle-in" doorway. And so, I had my entrance.

Another time, I chanced upon a section of glazed sewer tile with a chink knocked out of its bulbous end. Because the chink made room for a spout, my kettle neatly rested inside it. Let into the floor, next to my writing spot, the sewer tile became a hearth; my kettle had its place.

Opposite the writing shelf and hearth, I added an alcove for cooking. Dowels, set with space between them, formed half the alcove's floor so that water would pass through when I left bowls there, upside down, to dry.

These additions still left most of the hut free for sitting or for sleeping. But when the weather turned very cold, I built a sleeping loft spanning between the writing shelf and the sink alcove. Eventually I added two more alcoves along the remaining walls: one very low for a tiny wood stove, one slightly higher as an alternative to sitting on the floor.

As my dwelling took shape, it began to shape my life as well. And when I sat inside reading the recluse poets, the terse simplicity of their record framed my own perception, one I likened to a camera recording a world of pure experience. To deconstructionist philosophers, the idea of "pure experience" sets up a red flag; they think that pure experience presumes the authority of absolute or universal truth. But like Einsteinians who live their daily lives in a Newtonian universe, deconstructionists, too, lead private lives of pure experience. Only when such experiences construct a universal meaning for others—free of contingent time, place, and person—do deconstructionists have an edge to pick on, to pry loose.

For example, in a poem of constructed experience, Coleridge invests a simple leaf with not only sentience, but kin as well:

> The one red leaf, the last of its clan,
> That dances as often as dance it can,
> Hanging so light, and hanging so high,
> On the topmost twig that looks up at the sky.[19]

Dorothy Wordsworth also recorded the same vignette, but unlike her brother, William, and their friend Coleridge, Dorothy recorded the pure experience of it: "William and I drank tea at Coleridge's. A cloudy sky. Observed nothing particularly interesting—the distant prospect obscured. One only leaf upon the top of a tree—the sole remaining leaf—danced round and round like a rag blown by the wind."[20]

While constructed poems force the phenomena of the world into abstraction and ideal images, the poetry of pure experience yields to the relative concreteness of things. The recluse poet's pure experience presumes only immediate, relative, contingent authority. But I dwelt neither in the mountains of China nor in the Lake District of England, in neither the twelfth nor the nineteenth century. Instead, California's late-twentieth-century Sacramento Valley formed the world of my experience. In the years I had gazed out at a row of pomegranate trees at the rear of my yard, I never knew overripe pomegranates sometimes burst open. Reading in my hut one autumn evening, the sudden sound of a pomegranate cracking open riveted my attention.

One night when I went out to drink water from the garden tap, I heard a long-haul truck barreling along a distant freeway, and another time, as steam rose around my dishwater, I felt the floor rumble with a passing train.

These moments of immediacy made me shiver. I was unprepared for them. Even tent camping didn't approximate the hut's combination of fragile but permanent shelter, its amazing yet normally overlooked phenomena. The house whose backyard surrounded my hut, cocooned me from these perceptions. Only by placing my life in the midst of

Sink alcove, site of daily tasks and backstage for Tea

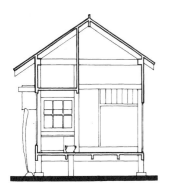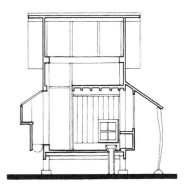

A proscenium of plywood over Tea's choreography

my backyard had I discovered its poetry. Like finding the firmness of scale through the placement of windows, I had found the commodity of my dwelling through the poetry of its use.

The reader familiar with Vitruvius may anticipate that the hut's third challenge will have something to do with delight, and may wonder why so obvious a construct as "firmness, commodity and delight" should guide a tale of pure experience. While the delight of the hut-dwelling poet is perhaps self-evident, in her moments of perception and poetry, that delight quickly vanishes with the arrival of others. Not *my* delight, but the delight of others formed my third and final challenge.

Crawling into the hut, guests always brought about the same result: the moments of delight—the bird perching to drink from water pooled on a rock, the play of shadows upon dusty windows, the wind scratching branches on the roof— all got lost in a cacophony of idle talk and chatter. About what? It didn't matter. Human beings close together *have* to talk; we're generally uncomfortable any other way. But in a theater, for example, we chatter madly to each other right up to the moment the curtain rises. Then, a wondrous thing happens. So long as action occurs on stage, we become silent as startled prey, intent upon looking and listening, just as happy to disappear.

One day, when I happened to sit where guests normally do, I noticed that the loft I used for winter-time sleeping suggested a proscenium overarching my own place, by the hearth and the kettle. At that point, I realized the full power of the tea ritual, a thing I had heretofore resisted because of its exoticism. But unlike rituals of other sorts, the tea ritual had nothing to do with meaning but everything to do with performance: the action on stage that stills the anxiety of humans huddled close upon one another.

I began to imagine what it might be like to be a guest there, to see a figure moving with slow, deliberate choreography. I imagined myself relaxing, awaiting the rest of the show. I imagined the moment the bowl would be put before me, when I too became a performer of slow and deliberate choreography, all the while taking in, as well, the sounds and sights of moments around me: birds, shadows, branches.

I filled in a small proscenium of plywood above the loft's beam, and I learned Tea's simplest choreography, sometimes called *obon date*. The first time I tried it out on others, it worked. As I glided the tea tray out from the sink alcove and made a deep bow, silence reigned: it was show time. And for twenty minutes, or maybe half an hour, we all played our parts, slowly coming to the point where conversation could begin: softly at first, in a different key—often of memory, at times of emotion.

If there was delight, it came from the willing suspension of social anxiety, and from discovering—as hut dwellers before us had—how it felt to dwell for a time in camera, where small window panes focused on the point where a tree trunk emerged from the ground, on the moment a falling leaf hit the earth.

The first hut had taken me six years to build, six years of trial by error perceived and then corrected. It is ironic, now, to find that what I thought happened instinctively might instead have been guided by my architectural training. Not consciously, of course; these classical categories are only explanation. But I have to wonder whether the habits these categories instilled in several generations of my teachers had not been instilled in me as well.

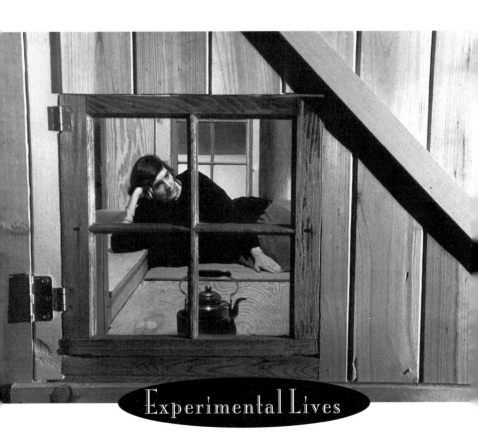

Experimental Lives

two

Before rational certainty flattened our perceptions, Francis Bacon (in 1594) recommended philosophers be set up with the following: "first, . . . a most perfect and general library . . . next, a spacious, wonderful garden [of divers plants, moulds, beasts, birds and fish] and . . . third, a goodly huge cabinet."[1]

This cabinet might have been a cupboard, or instead it might have been a room, what "cabinet" also meant in Bacon's time. In either case, this cabinet of curiosities formed the *theatrum mundi* of the humanists' circumscribed and centripetal world. In these cabinets one could have found "whatsoever the hand of man by exquisite art or engine has made rare in stuff, form or motion; whatsoever singularity, chance, and the shuffle of things hath produced; whatsoever Nature has wrought in things that want life and may be kept."[2]

In Italy, such "cabinets" might have been called *studiolo, guardaroba,* or, alternatively, the names that suggest their later evolution, *museo* and *galleria.* But at this stage, curiosity was uncatalogued and catholic. One might have found together shells, fossils, paintings, coins, bones, porcelain, roots, gems, and sculpture. This *theatrum mundi* embraced magic and erudition without distinction. It accumulated by "visible signs" and "signatures," and built from them an interpretation of *resemblances* and *sympathies.*[3]

At about the same time that Francis Bacon recommended a "goodly huge cabinet," the Jesuit missionary João Rodrigues—some years after Shuko's experiments—noted a parallel proclivity in the Japanese practice of *cha,* or Tea. In huts, like those of solitary hermits, followers of this regimen "give themselves over to the contemplation of the things of nature . . . [and] contemplate within their souls with all peace and modesty the things that they see there and thus

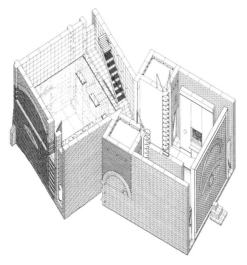

A "goodly huge cabinet" of visible signs and signatures
Credenza Curiosa, Opificio delle Pietre Dure, Florence

In huts for Tea, they contemplate the things of nature
Ennan teahouse, Yabunouchi Ennan, Kyoto, late sixteenth century

"I run across something . . . so I take it home and attach it"
Kurt Schwitters, *Merzbau,* Hanover, Germany, c. 1923

Castelli's exhibition catalogued the magma's new urgency
Taberna Ancipitis Formae, Rodolfo Machado and Jorge Silvetti, 1983

through their own efforts to understand the mysteries locked therein."[4] In the practice Rodrigues describes, like that of Bacon's humanist, nature was one vast single text: a "science" of signs and signatures, read from humble objects and natural phenomena and an "art" of resemblances and sympathies, read from seasonal and sensible juxtaposition. "Thus, from what they see in things themselves they attain by their own efforts to a knowledge of the First Cause."[5]

Later, seventeenth-century gentlemen turned their cabinet of curiosities inside out; the whole house and garden became a cabinet of rarities, combining the talismanic images of classical antiquity and the Garden of Eden. These gardens created a cosmos of plants, sculpture, and structure: a cabinet of the world.

Historians of rupture like to think that the rationalists made mincemeat of such humanist folly, but I think something else happened instead: again, as the rationalists picked the "easy apples" of semblance and sympathy to which the regular rules of universality and predictability might apply, artists stepped into the breach to replenish the diminishing supply of curiosity and astonishment. To insure that magic would not forever or in all cases lose to erudition, these artists sought every opportunity for amazement. In the garden, as a cabinet of the world, this amazement would be captured in the folly.

No better examples can be found than outside Paris, in the garden of Monsieur de Monville. An expert botanist, Monville collected a vast range of specimens for his study. But, the same garden housed an equally vast collection of sculpture and structure. By the time Monville completed his garden in 1789, aristocratic and bourgeois curiosity had established the folly garden as its new typology of curiosity, what Anthony Vidler has called a "kind of museum of meditative objects."[6]

Monville's folly collection included nearly all types then in vogue: a classical ruin, a broken column, a medieval ruin, a classical temple, a Chinese pavilion, a Tartar tent, an obelisk, a pyramid, a tomb, a rustic bridge, a thatched roof cottage, a hermitage, a dairy, an open-air theater, and a grotto. A cataloguer's nightmare, this *theatrum mundi* assembled a world of folly of which Monville and his guests formed the center. There Monville entertained not only Marie Antoinette and the duc d'Orleans, but Thomas Jefferson, as well.[7]

Nearly Laugier's contemporary, Monville's follies were to the humanist what Laugier's primitive hut was to the rationalist. Both men conjured structures of primary, or pared-down, habitation along with complex ideas about architecture and culture. Even so, the folly formed part of the humanist magma, ever churning below the surface of the rationalist landscape, and ready to erupt through any fissure of uncertainty. To the eighteenth-century rationalist, the folly builder might have appeared mad or merely exuberant, but beneath the skin, he or she was really still a humanist skeptic, too modest or too doubtful to embrace rational certainty alone.

This same magma, when it erupted on canvas, provided an endless source of mystery, curiosity, and astonishment. The art gallery became the greatest of all the cabinets of curiosity, endlessly dipping below the surface of its classical facade and pulling onto the surface those items that rationalists most longed to ignore—the visually distorted, the abstractly obscure, the baffling, the insulting, the erotic, the pornographic. These images appeared almost as if they were new geological or biological specimens found in an already well-catalogued world. Even today the mystery below rationalism still churns.

The Hamburg artist Kurt Schwitters may have best understood the gallery-as-folly. His *Merzbau*, begun in 1923, was less a cabinet of the world than a cabinet of the city. In a manner that would have delighted the instincts of Walter Benjamin, Schwitters's installation grew the way a big city does.

> I run across something or other that looks to me as though it would be right . . . so I pick it up, take it home, and attach it and paint it, always keeping in mind the rhythm of the whole. Then a day comes when I realize

I have a corpse on my hands—relics of a movement in art that is now passé. So what happens is that I leave them alone, only I cover them up either wholly or partly with other things, making clear that they are being downgraded. As the structure grows bigger and bigger, valleys, hollows, caves appear, and these lead a life of their own within the overall structure.[8]

Here, the final cubic order that Schwitters tried to evolve continually twisted and dissolved. The image of *white* magma erupting readily comes to mind. Moreover, while the caves and hollows suggest traditional folly antecedents, Schwitters's interest in the rhythm of the whole also suggests the sweeping purpose of a *theatrum mundi*, one that no longer searches for the Truth, but makes many truths instead.

The same magma of humanist doubt and uncertainty, having erupted in the follies of the eighteenth century and the paintings that would came later, reached the surface again in the late twentieth century—some through the architectural fissure of late modernism. On a hardened landscape of sterile geometrical repression, little eruptions of historic fantasy and regional longing began to appear, and one can almost understand "postmodern" design through the eruptions of its follies.

The most complete collection appeared in 1983, commissioned and exhibited by Leo Castelli in galleries in New York and Los Angeles. Nineteen architects—a kind of architecture who's who of the decade—presented architectural drawings and models of follies they devised as "a vehicle for commenting upon evolving ideas about architecture and urbanism, for advancing strongly held beliefs about systems of building, for incorporating narrative and fantasy, irony and wit."[9] In short, Castelli's exhibition catalogued the magma's new urgency, its preoccupations and proclivities: a Lantern that resembled a rocket (Peter Cook); a Broadway Folly of film devices—repetition, distortion, superimposition, and fading (Bernard Tschumi); a gigantic glass Fish and brick Snake (Frank Gehry); an Eroded Cube set on an elevated hypotenuse (Peter Eisenman/Jack Robertson); a nouveau classical Temple-House (Ricardo Bofill); a Thatched Tea Hut of modern and traditional materials (Arata Isozaki); and an Archetypal Pair of Primitive Huts, in sticks and stones (Michael Graves).

Some of these obviously continue previous folly preoccupations with the temple and the teahouse, while others introduce themes germane to our time alone; some are merely folly *objets* while others, like Machado and Silvetti's Taberna Ancipitis Formae, conjure a rich possibility of inhabitation. Still, all display an urgency to distill, within structures of primary enclosure, complex ideas about architecture and culture.

They are follies to be sure, and cabinets of "postmodern" curiosity, all.

Little Houses of Pleasure

If the Folly Exhibition of 1983 was catholic in its heterogeneity, the Osaka Follies of 1990 were protestant by comparison. Against the tide of Castelli's tolerant ambiguity, the Osaka Follies asserted heroic, almost intimidating forms; angularity prevailed over regularity, compositions of components won out over singular form, pretty historicism was out and earthy abstraction was in.

The product of a new phalanx of international designers that this time included Zaha Hadid, Coop Himmelblau, Morphosis, and Daniel Liebeskind, Osaka seemed to have struck a common chord absent in the follies of 1983, a chord that has erroneously come to be called "constructivist" (or, compounding the error, "deconstructivist").

How could this be? How could twelve designers from around the world produce work with so much in common that, had they all been constructed in a park without other structures around them, these follies might be taken for "cousins"?

Well, for all intents and purposes, both the idea of the park and its architectural language *had* already been introduced—in Le Parc de la Villette.

Constructed on the northeast fringe of Paris, a brief

carriage ride from Marie Antoinette's *hameau* and from Monsieur de Monville's folly garden, Le Parc de la Villette (1987) borrowed the idea of "little houses" set on a grid from Peter Eisenman's earlier Cannaregio Competition entry. In Villette, Bernard Tschumi also pushed Eisenman's tentatively "constructivist" theme, elaborating his cubist structures with elements of line: canopies, bridges, pergolas, stairs, and balconies.

This choice of a formal language for Villette's follies— one that actually harkened back to the Russian formalists— seems tentative because the formalists' work was so little understood that it was mistakenly called constructivist, another Russian movement entirely. With constructivism these follies bear little resemblance: a case, perhaps, of the arrière-garde posing in avant-garde drag.

Even so, the Parc de la Villette's greater lesson can be seen in the plan of its gardens. Villette's *folies* actually fulfill a complex program calling for theaters, galleries, and other places of resort and amusement. Tschumi housed these in separate pavilions, arranged in the open park along a strict grid. But to perambulate among them, one faces a series of meandering paths: what Tschumi called "cinematic" promenades, a device that recalled eighteenth-century gardens like those of the Marquise de Pompadour. Like Pompadour's avenues of pleasure and seduction, Tschumi's promenades employ curvilinear paths to cultivate the visitor's surprise.

At stake for Pompadour was keeping the king amused, and to this end she employed many devices: pageantry and spectacle, theatrical events under trellises or among mazes, and labyrinths or secret gardens sited behind gaps in the hedges. Her gardens included fountains where tritons, naiads, and cherub-bearing dolphins frolicked amid sprays and water jets. And too, she built pavilions in which she installed paintings by Boucher and sculpture by Pigalle, anticipating Catherine the Great's own hermitage, originally a small, private art gallery for the court's own amusement.

While the eighteenth century organized its gardens around pavilions, hermitages, and country retreats, eventually the spectacle of courtly amusements gave way to more private pursuits—centered around bathing, games of chance or skill, and finally around a single pleasure, with its own distinct altar: the "boudoir."[10]

In Paris, such little houses of pleasure came to be called "bagatelles," and many French aristocrats installed their mistresses in them. Diderot, in his *Bijoux Indiscrets*, describes a veritable mania for such little houses. Thus the formality of court life gave way to a private, libertarian quest for sensations that, no sooner provided, needed renewal from yet another turn of the path, yet another dissembled dalliance.

All these follies, gardens, and little houses of pleasure obeyed the rules of seduction; they provided what the eighteenth century required: "the dignity of order along with the promise of intimacy."[11] But whether boudoir or gallery, the pleasures of these little houses lay in their cohabitation. No longer a cabinet of curiosity or a *theatrum mundi*, the folly had become a *theatrum cupio*, an orchestrated seduction. The folly now served a Dionysian impulse loosely held within an Apollonian temple.

Nor was the Japanese tea man without his own pleasures. In the extreme, the boudoir and bath found expression in *rinkan chanoyu*, described as ribald parties that included drinking, bathing, and tea making. Shuko was associated earlier with this practice, and Shuko's Zen teacher, Ikkyu, was notorious for climbing over temple walls to spend his evenings in the pleasure quarter. Combined with other, more sedate origins, Tea found its eventual amalgam of intimacy and order within the practice of *suki*—simply translated, what one likes, what gives one pleasure.

For a very few, however, the path of *suki* was often paved with gorgeous intentions; the warlord Toyotomi Hideyoshi, for example, had a gold leaf–covered tearoom. For others, a new form—called *wabisuki*—provided a different, more chthonian pleasure:

For everything used in *wabisuki* is rough and mean; for example, the house is made of rough and old wood

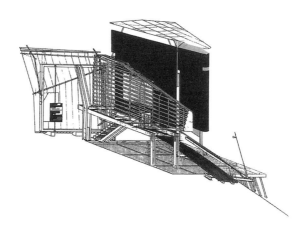

Such little houses of pleasure came to be called bagatelles
Chateau de Bagatelle, Abbeville, Somme, c. 1750

The anonymous spectator forms today's folly audience
Folly 2, Osaka, Architekturbüro Bolles-Wilson

An antiritual calling for righteousness and enthusiasm
Massachusetts campground cottage, c. 1860

Exhibiting grace under pressure, living generously and discreetly
Greyhound Bus Terminal, New York, 1947, photo by Esther Bubley

covered with straw and old reeds; earthenware caddies and vessels badly made with an artlessness and naturalness which seem to make them more ugly; earthenware cups to drink from . . . a path paved with rough stones . . . wild fruitless trees, and a wood with the ground covered with moss; an atmosphere of age; and many other things, all of them rough with no visible trace of splendour which might delight and please the senses.[12]

Even later forms of *suki*, which combined the artful with the artless, carried the memory of Tea's earthy experiments. The pottery of choice, Raku, was a rough-looking ware smooth to the touch. The character for *Raku* literally means "pleasure" and is the same character used in Lao Tzu's "taking *pleasure* [italics added] in his rustic tasks."

Were Thoreau not so little the aesthete, I would be drawn to indicate a parallel between the tea man's *suki* and Thoreau's life at Walden Pond. But Thoreau's intention—to live "deliberately," caged among the birds—makes his hut more a cabinet of curiosity than a little house of pleasure.

Instead, a lesser figure comes to mind. Called only Sue, she exists in an unlikely source, in M. F. K. Fisher's essay-as-cookbook, *How to Cook a Wolf*. Here Sue illustrates the author's point of view: that "it takes a certain amount of native wit to cope gracefully with the problem of having the wolf camp with apparent permanency on your doorstep."

> Sue lived in a little weatherbeaten house on a big weatherbeaten cliff. At first when you entered it, the house seemed almost empty, but soon you realized that . . . it was stuffed with a thousand relics. . . . lump-filled cushions that Whistler had sat on, and a Phyfe chair that had one stormy night been kicked into kindling wood by Oscar Wilde. . . . [Y]ou ate by one candle. . . . everything from one large Spode soup plate. . . . I have never eaten such strange things as there in her dark smelly room, with the waves roaring at the foot of the cliff. . . . The salads and stews she made from these little shy weeds [gathered from the cliffs and nearby fields] were

indeed peculiar, but she blended and cooked them so skillfully that they never lost their fresh salt crispness. She put them together with thought and gratitude, and never seemed to realize that her cuisine was one of intense romantic strangeness to everyone but herself. . . . Moreover, it was good.

The pleasure of Sue's "little . . . house" and her "inspired oblivion to the ugliness of poverty" appeals, "not because of its strangeness, but because of her own calm."[13] No Marquise de Pompadour, instead Sue was a *wabi* tea master in the New World. Even so, the pleasure of her little house, as with the "bagatelles" around Paris, lay in the intensity of its inhabitation.

But it is this very spirit of inhabitation that has gone out of the contemporary folly. Of the Osaka Follies, only Thom Mayne appears to have noted its absence: "To me the essence of architecture is to be found in its connection with daily life. . . . If I could make a criticism of the follies, it would be that in many cases they represent a detachment which may push them into the realm of 'sculpture.'"[14] No one inhabits follies anymore since the court no longer forms today's folly audience; instead, the anonymous spectator does.

The orderly deportment of the spectator guides us here, as we move along cinematic paths from formalist folly to formalist folly. Well-trained by decades of public inhabitation of what had once been the court's private realms—the gallery, the museum, the concert hall—here, now, we stroll not among acquaintances, but among strangers instead.

Entering these follies feels like entering an art gallery, where Thom Mayne's idea of "daily life" also seems quaint and distant. But daily life is only part of what we, as spectators, leave at the door; we leave behind our selves as well. Artist and writer Brian O'Doherty has observed: "The Spectator . . . consume[s] art . . . to nourish our nonexistent selves or to maintain some esthetic starveling called 'formalist man.'"[15] But while the well-trained "formalist man" dwells in the formalist folly gardens of Villette and Osaka, today this starveling may need more nourishment than that.

Ritual, Freedom, and Bondage

All cultures embroider themselves differently. Using the metaphors and symbols that, because of some timely need, just happen to catch on, all cultures invent rituals and practices of faith, or of form. Similarly, many cultures make room for their own contradiction. Whether the *heyoka*—the "sacred clown" of some Amerindian tribes—or the follies of certain European circles, viable cultures often include expression of their own deconstructing contradiction.

F.D.R. once said of an embarrassing ally, "He may be a son-of-a-bitch, but he's *our* son-of-a-bitch." In the case of emerging European modernism, *our* son-of-a-bitch was the folly, along with its rituals and practices. Contradicting modernism's rationalism and certainty, what was really at stake in the folly was freedom, modernism's irrepressible ally. For the humanist, the freedom of ambiguity in the face of certainty; for the romantic, the freedom of passion in the face of rationalism.

Taken together, the follies of curiosity and pleasure had no truck with ritual. Instead, they developed an "antiritual," what today we call "hanging out." The folly, and later the gallery, existed for dalliance and polite, petty conversation; the court and bourgeoisie "hung out" wherever they could stroll freely among points of interest and pleasure.

Even so, such antirituals call for a strict discipline. We only fool ourselves if we think such "freedom" is not shot through with a bondage equal to any monastic rite. To be casual and yet confident, amiable yet amusing in a milieu of social fluidity calls for a delicate play between the individual's will to power and the group's centrifugal force, its tendency toward conformity.

Paradoxically, the antiritual of the eighteenth-century folly well suited the emerging American spiritual agenda. The appearance of success and virtue that marked the elect sets a formal mode for even the most casual social encounter.

In this new world of spiritual materialism, conflating earthly and heavenly achievement, a person was no longer alone with his or her heavenly God or earthly confessor. Rather, one was on public exhibition. In place of the European display of courtly grace, Americans substituted the somber display of Puritan righteousness, and eventually the new dimension of enthusiasm as well.

In the 1840s, the Enthusiast Movement quickly influenced the American modus operandi. As the Enthusiasts melded with new mainstream religions, some developed their own severe follies in the camp-meeting grounds that dotted mid-nineteenth-century America. Originally comprised of only tents erected for religious revivals lasting several days, some revival camps, like Oak Bluffs on Martha's Vineyard or Lakeside in northern Ohio, became permanent communities. Church correspondence of the day called them "celestial cities." These theocratic burgs became realms of antiritual, calling for the "free" display of righteousness and enthusiasm twenty-four hours a day. As in the folly gardens of the Old World, every day was "Judgment Day," an opportunity for peer review.

No wonder, then, that the public realm that can be some people's heaven can be other people's hell. In parks and bistros, concert halls or church lobbies, the public collect in small knots of anxiety. While the elect love the audience of approval, the circumspect look for any chance to leave early. At the center of this seeming disparity lies the antiritual of freedom.

On the other hand the Chinese, under the influence of Confucianism, constructed their discipline of ideal social encounter, what they called *jen*. As in the folly's antiritual of freedom, a person expresses his or her *jen* in relationship to others. Even so, *jen* encompasses more than this; it involves a delicate balance between sociability and faithfulness to oneself. What's more, *jen* is neither opinionated, dogmatic, obstinate, nor egoistic. "While a wise man is free from doubts and a brave man is free from fear, a *jen* man is free from anxiety."[16] He moves among others with the character that African Americans call "cool": "To the degree that we live generously and discreetly, exhibiting grace under pressure, our appearance and our acts gradually assume virtual royal power. As we become noble, fully realizing the spark of creative goodness God endowed us with . . . we find the confidence to cope with all kinds of situations."[17]

From within and after the literal bondage of slavery, black American "cool" maintained the African (more specifically, Yoruban) legacy of *ashé*—a quality of spiritual command transcending ordinary social confinement and arrogance. *Ashé* and "cool," then, are the *jen* of the New World.

In the film *Six Degrees of Separation*, two couples exert their bragging rights over an experience they discover each shares: a young black man has insinuated himself among them (each couple in turn) by purporting to be a college friend of their respective children. In the milieu of other storytelling, the character played by Stockard Channing resists her husband's and her friends' efforts to demote the experience to the ranks of just another anecdote. She admires the poise of the stranger's benign deception, an authenticity of character that causes her to see empty deception among her own circle of friends.

Not by accident does the world of art and the gallery frame the characters of *Six Degrees of Separation*. In the gallery, the same tension divides authentic experience and cynical anecdote. But here dalliance and enthusiasm can turn especially mean. Retaining the righteous aggressiveness of the Enthusiasts' antiritual of freedom, the modern gallery has become the venue for what Brian O'Doherty has called the ritual of hostility. "Hostility to the audience is one of the key coordinates of modernism . . . [and] the semiotics of the hostility ritual are easily read. . . . For many of us, the gallery space still gives off negative vibrations when we wander in. Esthetics are turned into a kind of social elitism."[18]

Like the courtiers strolling the folly gardens of eighteenth-century France, or the faithful chatting in the revivalist campgrounds of nineteenth-century America, the gallery holds its audience in bondage by the severe demands of freedom. Judgment and anecdote, braggadocio and righteous conformism so bind this "freedom" that the passion with which modern people resist true ritual seems ironic.

By ritual, I am not adhering to the sloppy way in which almost anything from a cocktail party to brushing one's teeth becomes ritual to those who would enhance rituals' reputation by making them appear common. These are customs and habits; neither is ritual in the way that evokes modernist fear. We dismiss the bounded domain of ritual for the tightfisted freedom of modernity because, in our recoil from authority, we recall the wars waged against kings, princes, and popes— not to mention lesser-known personal grudges with nuns, priests, rabbis, or ministers. No wonder we run from ritual.

In ritual, not only do we do and say things we don't necessarily intend, but our performance goes sufficiently against the grain as to question our very identity. Moreover, ritual binds us so firmly that there appears no clear avenue of escape. But at stake in such rituals is another kind of freedom. Precisely because ritual so controls us, it demands that no personality or performance be conjured. In place of public judgment and its demands for apparently casual, even affable self-promotion, the bondage of ritual conjures a transcendent freedom.

This freedom appears especially obvious in the ritual of sado-masochistic bondage, where each partner acts out roles of domination or submission; the masochist orchestrates the scene while the sadist becomes his or her respectful servant. The more prescribed the interaction, the greater the freedom from self-invention, comparison, and competition. Literal bondage, here, is the *agent* of freedom and transcendence and, not unlike other bounded rites, the more prescribed the social interaction, the greater the freedom.

To achieve *jen*, Confucianists deemed essential various rites, or *li*. Originally sacrificial rituals, *li* became rules of proper conduct and decorum extended to a universal ethical system. By taking part in such a rite, participants gained a freedom within its boundaries that was, as with bondage, transcendent. Or, as in the bounded context of *ashé*, the chance to aspire to the coolness of grace under pressure.

We have already encountered the Japanese teahouse, as a cabinet of curiosity and as a little house of pleasure. But neither pleasure nor curiosity is as central to the teahouse as the concept of *li*. A rite of neither faith nor fact, the tea ritual explores *jen*, or what we might also call character or *ashé*. Within surroundings of material impoverishment and inverted, or upended, social hierarchy, the tea ritual provides an opportunity to achieve grace and elegance, bounded by the strict limits of choreographed decorum. Here the ritual completes the teahouse's *wabi* aesthetic, creating a contradictory world inside culture, a deconstruction of normal competition and striving.

In the tea ritual, the host attends to the guests—not simultaneously, but in turn regardless of social rank. This practice occasions polite bows, to those behind and ahead in turn. While bows frequently occur in Japanese society, with gradations that depend on rank, here not only are all bows equal but they extend to inanimate objects as well: the scroll and flowers displayed in the *tokonoma*, the kettle and hearth for boiling water, the tea bowl itself. Rather than establishing hierarchy, these wide-ranging bows acknowledge a generous arena of relationship and respect.

During tea making, while verbal exchanges are also prescribed, as with actors—simultaneously bound and freed by scripts—tea guests also summon the quality of their own expression, their *jen*, within and because of these limits.

When unprogrammed conversation begins, after the tea has been served and the tea utensils put away, this conversation arises as if out of a Quaker silence. The improvisation here occurs on a level quite different than had no ritual taken place. Having established a mode of mutual generosity among participants and objects, this conversation draws each participant's *jen*—his or her *ashé*—into play. Not unlike the riffs of jazz musicians, first bound by the drum's beat and intoxicated by its rhythm, tea conversations often take an unpredictable course, guests taking turns redirecting its flow the way jazz musicians sometimes do.

Like the juke joints of the Mississippi Delta, the teahouse's materiality also contradicts mainstream culture.

Made of rustic materials, common and close at hand, the teahouse and the juke joint both differentiate themselves from normative poverty as well. In the juke joint, bright colors applied to crude materials express a longing for the jazz salons of New Orleans (or even beyond that, for the dwellings of musical forebears in Haiti, or, earlier, the west coast of Africa). In the teahouse, the refined rusticity of *wabi* expresses a longing for the primitive huts of Japanese recluses (or, likewise beyond that, for the dwellings of poetic forebears in the mountains of China).

What the sacred drum is to the juke joint, the treasured tea bowl is to the teahouse. In either case, these primitive huts of jazz and of Tea enable their patrons to assume in the instant a "virtual royal power," making, as Okakura says of Tea, "all its votaries aristocrats in taste."[19]

Avant- or Arrière-garde?

So, whose term is the *avant-garde:* the artists' or their patrons'? Whose interest is served by a vanguard of the "new"? What army marches behind this front guard and where might it be headed? Since no one in stasis uses metaphors of progress, we must assume that "avant-garde" applies to those who would break a trail the rest of us will later widen; presumably the avant-garde holds the heroes, the geniuses of our future.

Progress had perhaps its last unambiguous fling in 1939, at the New York World's Fair. Besides introducing us to "balloon bread," the Fair heralded a visionary City of Tomorrow that was *rational, serious, pure, and safe*. But after the bombs of World War II wiped out many cities of its day, a new cycle of romanticism had its hearing. If Progress had left us vulnerable to a half-century of war's premature death, discomfort, and disease, then something was terribly amiss. As Europe rebuilt pieces of the City of Tomorrow on the ruins of war, a new avant-garde seemed to emerge with each new decade, almost like clockwork. In the 1950s, the absurd dethroned the logical; in the 1960s, camp dethroned the serious; in the 1970s, the hip dethroned the square; and in the

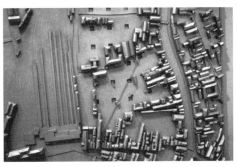

The juke joint differentiates itself from normal poverty
Tahaehe Horseman Club, Crawford, Mississipi, 1987, photo by Birney Imes

The opportunity for grace bounded by a choreographed decorum
Tea guests wait in garden arbor, photo by Takeshi Nishikawa

In the City of Tomorrow, a new avant-garde emerged with each decade
General Motors City of the Future, New York World's Fair, 1939

The hut, as folly or pavilion, has spontaneously appeared as a leitmotif
Peter Eisenman's Cannaregio Competition entry, 1978

1980s, deconstruction dethroned the pure. Now, in the 1990s, the uncanny is dethroning the safe and secure.

But, slashing their way to progress, these avant-gardes of progress have had to contend with Rousseau. They have had to lead an assault on Clarens, and disrupt the reverie of *Héloïse*. That no one reads Rousseau's only novel anymore does not diminish its influence on us. A curious utopian vision of pastoral simplicity, resource recycling, and simmering passion, Clarens was on the mind of nearly every eighteenth-century reader; Marie Antoinette was only the most famous. Countering the threat of technological progress, Clarens defined an alternative choice—a world that could be, but whose opportunity would soon be lost. Clarens didn't embrace Nature unbridled, a position that later, Romantic apologists for Nature would slip into; instead it promoted an intentional contract with nature.

To the army of Progress, Nature was the enemy, but to Rousseau, the enemy was the very army of Progress itself. Rousseau set a rear guard in motion, an arrière-garde of intense irritation and, later, uncertain direction. From the untamed wilderness of Coleridge, Wordsworth, and Turner, to the primitive and psychological romanticisms of Matisse, Gauguin, Picasso, Freud, Bacon, and Le Corbusier's Ronchamps, and to the abstract romanticisms of Mondrian and Le Corbusier's La Tourette, Rousseau's arrière-garde has always resisted the army of Progress. To make this apparent, although sometimes ridiculous, all have seen themselves in some way or another as an avant-garde.

But so long as Nature dealt out discomfort, disease, and premature death, the real avant-garde of Progress forged a path of machines and medicines that, understandably, society has been willing, on the whole, to follow. Neither the Luddites nor the Unabomber could turn this army around.

In the eighteenth century, the receding significance of aristocratic patronage led to a new cutting edge in the arts and architecture; by the nineteenth century, the arts had a new, burgeoning bourgeois audience in the aristocrats' place. But before too long, artists felt the same irritation with the bourgeoisie that they had felt in the service of their aristo-cratic patrons. In our own time, we do not speak of bour-geois culture anymore. Instead we have a mass audience that irritates us.

Even though the customs of progress have always prized ground-breaking genius, each of the recent avant-gardes has shocked or confused. Not only had artists hit targets the middle class could not see, but they aimed their volleys, as rearguard skirmishes frequently do, to redirect, not further the march. But unlike the avant-garde early in this century, with its broad ethical and populist components, these artists and architects were supported by a new fame system—one that found salable anything different and new, no matter how shocking (or because of it). Thus, by the laws of genius and differentiation, this postwar avant/arrière-garde merely dec-orated the supply train and entertained the troops. Doomed to decades of rearguard scuffles, it produced stars but no heroes.

Today, avant-garde young Turks, that phalanx who think of themselves as a cadre, seek the fame of genius from the shock of the uncanny. Even so this target may be more vis-ible and more commonly understood, today, than they think. The contemporary condition of hypercompetition that ren-ders so many lives insecure may be more *nourished* by experi-ences that evoke fight or flight than they are undermined by them. But, the ubiquity of uncanny images in advertisements or the glitzy coverage of architecture fever suggests that to-day's geniuses may be at work somewhere else, on some other target not so easily perceived. Rousseau's real revolu-tionaries might be those who build the primitive huts and shacks of a different City of Tomorrow on the margins of every city of today.

As we approach the twenty-first century, with a rich array of millennial disasters before us, the hut—as folly or pavilion—has spontaneously appeared as a *leitmotif* in recent building—from Eisenman's Cannaregio to Tschumi's Parc de la Villette, from Circuit City to Seaside. One wonders why. Are such follies and pavilions merely the whimsical product of client or architect escapism? Or do they serve other, deeper impulses of curiosity, pleasure, experimentation, or discipline?

In other times of cultural transition, the primitive hut, as invention or as a construct of experience, has brought humans to the edge of their normative existence and, from there, allowed perspective and experimentation. The more "primitive" the hut, the more its creators recognized the arbitrariness of their own culture.

In his time, Herodotus produced the same effect when he relayed the tales he'd been told of bizarre cultural practices, even within close geographic proximity to the world he embraced as his norm. As the modern world becomes more homogeneous, the perspective we might gain from such comparison becomes more difficult, even as the norm itself shifts. While the primitive hut belongs equally to "what architecture is" as to "what architecture is not," ironically, its greatest significance may derive from the many nonarchitectural ideas it engages. Within the inhabited hut, cultural issues and practices readily converge. With an agility larger structures can never match, huts bring together the physical environment with such disparate aspects of culture as necessity, fantasy, faith, and "life-style." The hut, then, may be humankind's supreme experiment.

Interval

The Hut in the Rotunda

In a small college town, a rotunda rises from a massive circle of dreary brick. Above second-floor balconies and past four plaster-covered arches, the rotunda rests, at last, on a circular drum. Sixteen windows pierce the drum, each bearing an illustrious name: Dante, Newton, Lincoln, Goethe; Bach, Plato, Darwin, Carlyle; Bacon, Paul, [Michael] Angelo, Cicero; Emerson, Homer, Hugo, and even Froebel (the educator whose blocks were Frank Lloyd Wright's playthings). At the turn of the nineteenth century, *architecture* was brick, earthbound, while *art, theology, science,* and *philosophy* remained up among the angels.

For nearly fifty years, this apotheosis in angelic plaster and chthonian brick marked the entrance to a university library. Here, through two world wars and the boom and bust that connected them, students checked out books (and each other), hushed by the aura of monumental space and the memory of great men. By the 1960s, the library abandoned its structure for a new, larger neo-Georgian warehouse that had been built nearby. No aura there; no apotheosis.

Meanwhile, the university turned over the empty old library, with its brooding rotunda, to a slightly embarrassed architecture faculty, some of whom would have preferred a real warehouse of steel, glass, exposed trusses, and the like. Even so, the architects quickly occupied all the old library . . . almost.

When I decided to rebuild the hut I had built in California, one of the second-floor balconies below the rotunda's arches turned out to be the only space available. Scarcely larger than the hut would be, the balcony provided an inspiring workshop, a glen of cool silence within the buzzing heat of a midwestern summer. My assistant John and I discovered that what might have been a fairly prosaic job of carpentry became, in the rotunda's templelike quiet, a kind of meditation. By tacit agreement, we spoke rarely as we cut and fit ordinary plywood and two-by-fours to the specifications of

A balcony beneath one arch provided an inspiring workshop

An underground life emerged around the hut

memory. We finished the hut just before the students returned in the fall.

Unnoticed at first, the hut soon became the object of curiosity. Incongruously tiny, inside a grand monumental space, the hut was not unlike a baldachino over a cathedral's altar, or a temple's *huppah* awaiting a bride and groom.

Gradually, however, I detected a kind of underground life emerging around the hut and a lore of habitation connected to it. In a storage place, I found a neatly folded army blanket: "To cover up with when I come here to crash," someone said. One day, I discovered notes for an exam. Another time, I found a poem, begun in one hand and continued in two others. Strangers? Friends? I didn't know which. Throughout the day and into the night, the hut became a frequent rendezvous—for teaching assistants grading papers, for studio partners comparing schemes, for couples catching a private moment. I even learned that a common student fantasy had been to "get laid" in the hut, although I never found out if anyone ever fulfilled this desire. Most typically, however, students came there just to sit. As one student explained it: "Your hut takes me to someplace else."

While I had intended only to craft an artifact and use it occasionally for tea, the hut's public venue turned it into a statement. Not surprisingly, therefore, not all comments were kind; one colleague, whose office looked out onto the rotunda, complained of having to look at it. But to the students, the hut was a pleasure. It didn't resist any idea or use they thought of.

Instead, the hut projected the strange attraction of its frank admission: that in the midst of the severely exercised minds and egos filling the studios arrayed below it on all sides, something else existed beyond the crushing tradition of classical or avant-garde architecture. The hut was not beautiful, nor aggressive; not even clever. All the same, the hut was a well-crafted thing, difficult to dismiss. In a word, the hut was *homely*, and precisely this plain unpretentiousness was what people either hated or loved. Because it moved them in ways that architecture seldom did, the hut escaped

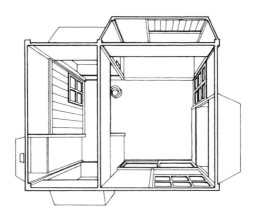

A well-crafted thing, difficult to dismiss

architecture's presumptuous fraternity and the specter of competitive rivalry. In the middle of an architecture school, this hut provided a free zone, a place out of bounds.

Meanwhile, to me, the hut only wanted to be outdoors. Inside it, I could recall the trees that once sprung from the earth outside its windows, a memory that grew insistent as spring approached. Fortunately, the opportunity for the hut's removal came with a summer phone call. The actor Jodie Foster was directing her first movie and wanted the rotunda as a location. The only problem was the hut. The camera crew couldn't shoot around it. "Could we lose it?" they asked. "How much would that cost?"

A year or two later, after the hut had been dismantled, moved, and reerected outdoors, I saw the movie *Little Man Tate*—the one that had caused some disappointment to students who returned the next year to find "their hut" had disappeared. As I watched the film, I felt the sensation of familiarity when I saw doors that I recognized, and then in a smooth swirl, the camera panned around the rotunda.

And that was it: five seconds you'd miss if you spilled your popcorn or stifled a sneeze. After rounding the rotunda, the camera brought the viewer to a grand doorway I didn't recognize and through it to an elegant, wood-paneled room that I did not recognize either. The camera's path was smooth and believable, even though it told a lie.

I had never before experienced behind the scenes what the film industry calls "production values," the collage of tasty bits remade into fictitious reality. The effect, I admit, was wonderful, but also depressing. We had removed our hut for no more than a bit of atmosphere.

I am a hut builder. Compared to a filmmaker, I work in an unglamorous medium. I work with "ordinary reality." But how, I wondered, can this reality be defended in the face of such convincing and seductive images? Or did the rivalry begin the other way around? When monumental architecture made reality grand, did the film tinkerer not wonder what light, celluloid, and action could do to rival such architectural splendor? Dim the lights and ordinary reality disappears. Project a sequence of images and a substitute reality takes its place.

While the architect takes monumental reality as his stock-in-trade, and uses it to arrest the beholder's attention, diminutive space gets our attention too. Architectural space, however large or small, joins and then bends attention to new thoughts, to a heightened consciousness. Even so, it is really action—whether in film or in architecture, whether the formal rituals of Mass or the more intimate rituals of huts—that captures us.

W. C. Fields said that the best thing about movies was that they moved. Zen patriarch, Hui-neng, said of a flag fluttering in the wind that it is not the wind, not the flag, but the *mind* that moves. The mind arrested by movement steps out of its ambling stream of consciousness. Only when combined with the diminution or monumentalization of architectural scale does the medium of place and ritual rival the movies and the other spectacles of culture.

In the rotunda of an architectural school, an unannounced hut beckoned all comers to the margins of architecture. Under a monumental arch of one architectural tradition rested an opposed tradition: the primitive hut and all that follows from it. The hut in the rotunda invited sexuality, poetry, sleep, or contemplation.

Of course the hut had to give way to the movie camera. Not only was the hut in the way, the hut was redundant; it was, in and of itself, a camera. The hut focused our experience of shelter and our ideas of culture, illuminating what might really be at stake beneath the level of common perception.

Ritual Intentions

three

Vision(s)

To examine so many points of cultural intersection—Asian, European, and American—I have had to let most of each one's context fall by the wayside. What has remained may only be a semicoherent pattern of huts, shacks, follies, and teahouses, along with the rituals and antirituals of their inhabitation. Even so, to account for the present—still quite liquid—can be the most difficult of all.

Take for example two avant-garde teahouses, recently constructed along with three more traditional ones on the UNESCO plaza in Paris. The first, "Flowery/gaudy Teahouse" by Tadao Ando, looks like a huge bottle gourd. Entirely white, inside and out, Ando's teahouse reminded one reviewer, Atsushi Miyatani, of *A Clockwork Orange* or *2001: A Space Odyssey.*

The second, "One-more-time Moon/Month," has a gigantic red balloon on top that appears to hold the structure's transparent walls apart. From the outside, the ceremony behind these walls—actually two parallel panes of heavy glass with sand in between—looked like tropical fish suspended in a tank. Moreover, Miyatani suggests, "between guest and master exists a feeling of serious tension. When, what hour will the interdependence of the glass and the balloon collapse?"[1]

What shall we make of these teahouses and the uneasy impressions they create? Does it help to know that the exhibition's producer, Hiroshi Teshigahara, also created a structure from hundreds of pointed stakes, or many years earlier had directed a film of similarly uncanny impressions: *The Woman in the Dunes*? And what does Teshigahara tell us in the exhibition's pamphlet, where he draws a parallel between this 1993 event in Paris and the Grand Tea Gathering of 1587, at Japan's Kitano Shrine?

There, at the order of the warlord Hideyoshi, all the tea masters of Japan gathered to demonstrate their individual,

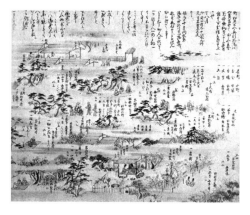

Tadao Ando's bottle-gourd shaped teahouse recalls **A Clockwork Orange**
Large Tea Meeting, UNESCO Plaza, Paris, 1993, photo by Atsushi Miyatani

Eventually twelve hundred tea huts and shelters filled the shrine's pine groves
The Grand Kitano Tea Gathering of 1587, painting by Ukita Ikkei

Baselitz is the artist; the teamaker can only be an assistant
Georg Baselitz's studio near Hamburg, c. 1983, photo by Ken Probst

Such intimate rituals as tea engender common vision and participation
The host himself prepares tea, photo by Takeshi Nishikawa

idiosyncratic visions of tea making. Eventually some twelve hundred tea huts and shelters filled the shrine's pine groves for what Hideyoshi planned as a ten-day event. Made of thatch and mud plaster, or paper screens and simple roofs, the tea huts and shelters at Kitano evoked impressions of harmony, respect, purity, and tranquillity, a quartet of qualities later codified by the Japanese tea ritual. As a collection of independent visions we know now from diary accounts, and even some paintings, we sense a common thread at Kitano, nearly a shared vision: not miniatures of a grand aristocratic or monastic tradition, instead these tea huts replicate the huts we see in Chinese paintings or read about in accounts like Kamo no Chomei's.

At Kitano, life itself provided the only uncanny note. Hideyoshi ended the gathering after just one day to turn his attention, it is said, to a rebellion in Kyushu.

Even so, the vision of Tea at Kitano lasted well beyond Hideyoshi himself and would eventually come to center the making of a culture during rocky times ahead. The vision of *wabi*—of rustic yet refined poverty—would refract all that might be projected onto it into a myriad of related arts and crafts. In short, the tea ritual bound the Japanese people together, permitting them all to participate in this common vision.

In the West, the "vision of art" has recently taken on an alternate and often more dominant meaning: *vision as sight*, or the representation in two dimensions of what the eye perceives from three. From the draftsman's calculated scribings to the impressionist's demonstration of sight's emotion to the color theorist's hard-edged sciencelike visual experiments, modern artists have made a shared vision out of sight. A painting, for example, may more often be about the act of seeing than about subject or narrative, and artists presume their audience floats in abstract appreciation, as so many "disembodied eyes." Until only recently, we have taken for granted the other sense of vision that this implied: the shared vision of modernity. This vision looked to new inventions, new styles, and an accumulating list of geniuses who hit targets no one else could see, or have any use for, until the impresario or the critic made them clear and indispensable.

But at some point, this vision of modern progress and modern art exhausted itself. Art critic Donald Kuspit questions: how can art put us in touch with the "higher" when we no longer have faith in the "higher"; when disillusionment with art expresses itself as mocking with no offer of replacement; when art feeds on other art, making both seem gratuitous and dispensable; or when art no longer serves thought or feeling and, like a shell left on the shore of discourse, is inhabited in the manner of a sand crab.[2]

Moreover, to Kuspit, avant-garde models of art have lost their ability to be radical, or to reinvent art. In postmodern art, any choice becomes just one among many, all equally valid. In place of fame, we only have celebrity, and personal expression has become impersonal performance, be it "playful" or "chic"—a kind of exhibitionistic "flashing" with no significance. Avant-garde ideas about art have run out of steam. Instead we have a "neo" world—of neorealism, neo-conceptualism. There is even a neo-avant-garde, where works are faked, forced, or manipulated. Images have become normative, routine, and reduced to common denominators; they have lost their mystery, becoming "Hollywoodized" and "kitsch-ified." Meanwhile, we have modern depression at its greatest extreme, a depression that comes from the loss of vision and the fact that vision has come to be absurd in the modern age. "Sherrie Levine says to Julian Schnabel, 'I didn't know anybody still believed in that.'"[3]

For others, the problem's source is obvious. Suzi Gablik writes, "Our way of thinking about art [has become conditioned] to the point where we have become incredibly addicted to certain kinds of experience at the expense of others, such as community, for example, or ritual. . . . Not only does the particular way of life for which we have been programmed lack any cosmic, or transpersonal dimension, but its underlying principles [have become] manic production and consumption, maximum energy flow, mind-less waste and greed."[4] For Kuspit, society no longer needs an artistic avant-garde. What society needs instead is an ethical avant-garde, that is, "a vision that affords perspective on our existence and the hidden aspirations of man."[5] What Kuspit and Gablik, both, may really be saying is that the avant-garde needs (once again) to become ethical.

In 1993, inside a large exhibition hall in Tokyo's Harajuku district, five contemporary architects constructed five different teahouses, each subsequently used for tea rituals. The first teahouse, a bold lace of scrap iron covered with rust, literally interprets the exhibition's theme of *sabi*, or the aesthetic of agedness, the spirituality of patina. Two other teahouses combine sections of bamboo screen with translucent or opaque paper, allowing the gallery's light to illuminate the interior. The first of these recalls Mondrian's *Salon de Madame B. à Dresden* in the way views of the gallery surrounding it play with the planes that enclose. The other, long and narrow, has at its center a log, planed smooth on the top. Tea utensils rest at one end and guests sit, not on the floor, but on a couch. The fourth is the simplest but also, perhaps, the most arresting: a plain cubic frame stands beside a bench made from a thick, clear acrylic board resting on a thicket of stainless steel rods. Even though its bold execution suggests quiet calm, it resists any impression of sweet preciousness; this teahouse is of its time.

Still, the last, "Heaven's Hut" by Masayuki Kurokawa, is not only the most daring but probably also carries the strongest sense of Tea's contemporary vision. Two long, parallel walls, of a large-grain, woven, linenlike fabric face one another. Guests sit along the curved wall and face the wall that is flat, backlit, carrying on its surface the computer-animated video image of a white flower petal floating on a shallow pool. To the side rest utensils for tea making—a heterodox collection of pottery, metal, lacquer, and bamboo. Sitting there, one reviewer, Yasuyuki Ogura, noted how easily one lost track of time. Of the entire collection, Ogura said, "It has given me an impression of fresh surprise and tranquillity."[6]

At opposite ends of the globe, this exhibition and the one in Paris form a new vision, a new Kitano. Each exhibition recognizes its audience's addictions and exhaustion, its inability to revisit tradition innocently. Even so, each takes the tea ritual's choreography seriously, as a mode of inhabitation, so that these places will enchant without sentimentality. Taken together, these exhibitions suggest one direction, perhaps the best direction, for anyone interested in an ethical avant-garde.

I recall a photograph of the artist Georg Baselitz on the floor of his studio. Baselitz sits in classic Tea *seiza*, resting on his knees, a painting spread before him. At the rear, a second person stands, pouring water from a kettle into a teapot. In the West, only Baselitz is the artist; the tea maker, who might also be an artist, at the moment of the photograph can only be a friend or an assistant.

In the tea tradition, *both* can be artists—one of paint, the other of tea.

For reasons that are complex but not coincidental, an activity patterned to be like the Japanese tea ritual might offer advantages to anyone interested in the idea of an ethical avant-garde. Because Tea unites maker and viewer in a commonly shared experience, the product of tea making is not separate from the process of its production. Artist and audience share the same moment of creation. By contrast, a painter paints and later, in the gallery's neutral, abstract environment, the viewer sees that product unrelated to the circumstances of its creation but related only to other curiosities, other "specimens."

What appears to be ceremonial—and, to the modern mind, potentially tied to mumbo jumbo—is rather a choreography of silence and sound, like the pauses between action and speech. But from the point of view of each participant's experience, ritual allows each to enter the event. Ritual eases the anxiety between the self and the other, allowing "those who cannot will themselves out of the secular to perform the spiritual, as dancing allows the tongue-tied man a ceremony of love."[7]

Compared with the "ritual of hostility" that O'Doherty finds in the gallery, such intimate rituals as tea engender common vision and participation. Like Confucian rites, these rituals offer a shared vision of space and time; they elicit not only the "hidden aspirations of man" generally, but the *jen* or "coolness" of each participant individually. While such rituals won't make anybody rich or famous, they may cause those ambitions to matter very little.

Uncanny Arts and Untenured Lives

If Tea is tranquil, pure, and harmonious, then it is so only in contrast to the uncanniness of the world around it. In the midst of a frightening world, Tea establishes a homely calm, the mirror opposite of a horror story read in a cozy room.

Anthony Vidler suggests that modern culture's taste for the uncanny is "the pleasure principle afforded by a terror that was, artistically at least, kept well under control."[8] But the opposite taste—for the homely—has been a constant as well. In a world of nuclear weapons, holocausts, and environmental disasters, Hollywood movies must end happily in case life itself does not. A good bit of our culture embroiders human hope into scenarios that eke out large and small beneficences from a hostile or indifferent world.

The greatest genius of Tea, Sen no Rikyu, squarely set his homely target within the uncanny world of his patron, the warlord Hideyoshi. Teshigahara (of *The Woman in the Dunes* and UNESCO tea exhibition fame) opens his film, *Rikyu*, with a well-known story. Hearing that Rikyu's tea garden is covered in morning-glory blossoms, Hideyoshi makes fast tracks to see the glorious sight. Ahead of time, Rikyu plucks just one blossom, places it in the tea hut's *tokonoma* and has all the remaining blossoms cut away. This gesture confuses Hideyoshi, a simple man of gratuitous violence. Crestfallen, and not much amused by this lesson, like a serial killer about to run amok, he manages to make Rikyu's homely hut as uncanny and chilling as he makes the entire world around him—a world of insane plans to conquer

China, of exile, murder, and ordered suicides (including, ultimately, Rikyu's).

Today, too, finds interplay between islands of secure calm within a relatively uncanny world but, likewise, islands of the uncanny within a generally secure world. It all depends on one's point of view.

For some people, these *canny* islands are more attainable than for others. The modern hope has always been that someday there would be security enough for all, and well there might be. But for the foreseeable future, the world is divided between those whose lives appear secure and those whose lives do not. For the unsecured, the uncanny forms islands of refreshment within this culture's canny and hope-filled scenarios; these are the lives nourished by such uncanny visions as the unsettling UNESCO teahouses in Paris.

But why, Vidler seems to ask, do these uncanny sensibilities appeal right now, "erupt[ing] in . . . the wasted margins and surface appearances of postindustrial culture."[9] Why do our arts more frighten than calm us? Is there some connection between these uncanny arts and the hypercompetition that renders so many lives insecure? Are competitive lives more nourished by experiences that evoke fight or flight than by experiences that calm and comfort?

A full exegesis of the parallel circumstances of uncanniness and competition lies beyond our interest here. However, some aspects of the connection between the uncanny in art and the untenured lives of its audience may help place primitive huts and their ritual intentions—if they have a place at all—in the world as we find it.

Typically those of us who lead secure, tenured lives—with careers in teaching, clergy, civil service, and the military; or, to a lesser degree, in monopolized and selective professions, like law and medicine; or finally, who are self-tenured by inheritance or frugal management—we tenured form the *canny arts'* primary audience. Even so, we also appreciate the uncanny, though most often historic rather than current, embodied in the past avant-gardes of music, arts,

Sen no Rikyu set his homely target within an uncanny world
Taian-Myokian, late sixteenth century, Kyoto

A steely exterior behind its mocking picket fence
Dennis Hopper house, Venice, California, c. 1990

and literature that extend the cultural canon's continuity and prolong its conversation. We admire those heroes; their vision inspires us.

Meanwhile, the unsecured—those who are "downsized," "reorganized," reemployed as "consultants" or in "temp" jobs—discover a degree of competition once thought to end after school, as it may have for our parents. Because competition tends to privilege the energy and drive of adolescence over the maturity and judgment of adulthood, the untenured seek experiences that boost energy over those that unwind it. When next week's paycheck depends on being "up" right now, "dosing"—whether from the rush of aerobic, chemical, or uncannily induced adrenaline—may suggest less an escapist than a competitive strategy.

Uncanny artifacts and architecture—brutal, erotic, frightening—are ill explained, then, without reference to the essential condition of the competitively insecure. The ability of these uncanny things and places to keep one "on edge" makes them nourishing. If they form a style, it has less to do with their aesthetic evolution or their formal characteristics than with what these appearances *supply* to the lives of the insecure. Add to this those who, in spite of actual or virtual tenure, just plain like the competitive life for its "kick"—the intelligentsia that dabbles on the "cutting edge"—and you find the constituency for this decade's uncanny culture; you find its signature, its essence.

The steely exterior of Dennis Hopper's house—behind its ironic, mocking picket fence—may be paradigmatic for our age. Nothing about this house is homely; its exterior is chillingly severe, fearful, alien, unsettled—uncanny. We do know that its owner, a film actor (and like all actors, only as good as his last performance and his current rating) ended years of drug dosing just before—we are told—it would have killed him. Still, the need to be "up" for the next role, and the one after that, suggests that the house's chilly foreboding forms a kind of architectural methadone, sustaining but not life-threatening.

Meanwhile this house that doses also shields; we assume

that its owner would be tough, like its exterior. But for all we know, the Hopper inside may be turning lamp stands on a lathe and listening to *The Sound of Music*. The point of the uncanny exterior is that we cannot know. We can only assume that its owner is as virile, energetic, and aggressive as the house itself. In this sense, the picket fence protects far more than its physicality suggests; it protects certainly more than it might in an *Ozzie and Harriet* venue. Because the fence "protects" the incorrigible house with sweetness, it mocks its own function. Doing so, it also mocks our fantasies of security. If the house is a bully, then the fence kicks sand in our face. The competition going on here is a mind game whose victories come by causing our hidden longings to become as a twisted piece of shrapnel, already inside us, now turned against our sense of well-being.

Our cultural tastes sharply divide those things that, on the one hand, promote the values of comfort and security from those that, on the other hand, inspire us in a world of prolonged competition. Even so, the term *uncanny* belongs to tenured discourse. Who else classifies things as uncanny but those who hold the canny dear. To the tenured, then, the uncanny is the absence of "high" culture's values and virtues, while the uncanny opposes the values of the tenured: humility, charity, and chastity, among others.

Those familiar with Nietzsche may have already jumped to the chase. The virtues I associate with the culture of tenure, Nietzsche calls the virtues of the *slave*. Institutions grant tenure, after all, in return for servitude of some sort and often withhold it for lack of collegiality—that is, charity and humility accorded one's colleagues. Or later, these same institutions can revoke tenure—most often, nowadays, for breaches of chastity we call sexual harassment.

By contrast, the virtues Nietzsche attributes to the *slave's master*—competitive rivalry, independence, spontaneity, and sensuality—also belong to the insecure whose uncanny arts valorize these traditionally aristocratic virtues. The independent hero is ubiquitous in uncanny film—from *On the Waterfront* to *The Road Warrior*, and the spontaneously sensual artist dominates music and art—from Elvis Presley to Kurt Cobain, from happenings to raves.

But is this a world of values turned upside down, or merely two worlds of value, separate but not equal? They would not be equal, not because untenured values don't exist but because, as Bernd Magnus notes, "most of Western humanity knows no other values than those associated with an asymmetrically hierarchically dualistic, binary ascetic ideal." That is, we in the West divvy up virtues—plus and minus—to favor those that are canny. For this reason, redividing the virtues—between those that truly help human lives and those that do not—outlines a "cultural transvaluation of staggering proportions,"[10] as staggering as the task of reassigning gender to all Romance-language and German nouns, for example.

In such a transvaluation of virtue, one must decide what part of the uncanny's independent, spontaneous sensuality one wishes to include, and as well, what portions of the canny's chaste and charitable humility one wishes to exclude. What dosing helps and what dosing hurts? In normal situations, transvaluation *is* staggering. But such processes of reversal and revaluation are what the primitive huts of cultures with history and architecture are especially good at. The primitive hut can transvalue culture because no pre-existing rules or categories govern it. As Lyotard says of such experiments, "[These] rules and categories are what the work . . . itself is looking for."[11]

The folly drawings in Leo Castelli's exhibition and the built follies at Osaka already suggest such hut experiments. But with no inhabitation more engaged than the exhibition-goer's disembodied eye, we merely have a gawking crowd in the midst of a spectacle. We do not have a discourse that can judge on any other basis than that of pure form, already well established in the formal values of modern asceticism and its reluctance to engage physical, human presence. But once a folly has its habitués, accustomed to frequent, physical inhabitation, we have a group who can gauge the folly's experiment as it progresses, who can comment and judge.

Just such a group surrounded Rikyu in his time. Guests of each other's experiments, these tea men noted the relative merits of the *sakui* (invention) and *mitate* (discovery of new value in things previously overlooked or taken for granted) each tea man employed. Over time, such judgments formed a new canon and a new system of values. Eventually this avant-garde action became so well known and caught on with so many that it displaced the cultural dominance of all previous norms. Tea, then, was once a process of transvaluation, and one of staggering proportions. In the midst of courtly values, these tea men formed, over several generations, what Richard Rorty might call a "contingent community."[12] We can now speak of Rikyu's genius, rather than of his eccentricity or perversity, because his private obsession hit a target others had use for. It was a deep personal statement made universal by his own discipline.

The cultural experimenter in architecture and in ritual (that is to say, in inhabitation) who wants to know how uncanny sensibilities transvalue the norm need only build a small slice of habitation to posit his or her vision. Meanwhile, we are already running another experiment—one started long ago by others but one we must attend to nevertheless: the experiment of sustaining 5.7 billion persons in the processes of industrializing an entire planet. Just as our primitive hut and its ritual experiments rely on a contingent community of judgment, our very experiment itself relies on this other, planet-focused one. Or, perhaps it could be all the same experiment, run at two different scales.

Inside the Stretch Limo

Environmentalist Thomas Fraser Homer-Dixon has asked us to "think of a stretch limo in the potholed streets of New York City, where homeless beggars live. Inside the limo are the air-conditioned post-industrial regions of North America, Europe, the emerging Pacific Rim. . . . Outside is the rest of mankind, going in a completely different direction."[13]

Inside the stretch limo, when we're not worried about terrorism or violence, everyone worries about ecology. Out-

What if the stretch limo were to become America's experimental hut?
Edward and Nancy Reddin Kienholz, *The Caddy Court*, 1986–1987

side the stretch limo, the rest of mankind worries first about food and shelter, water and land. But when they can, they dream of something better. To the degree that those outside the stretch limo encounter Western mass media, their dreams may be conflicted: between historic, regional, ethnic visions of "the good life" and dreams of modernity's bounty instead.

Such dreams have an accompanying economy that goes something like this: some of us in the stretch limo trade baubles for the resources and cheap labor of those outside. Later, others come back with TVs and VCRs that they trade for more resources, more labor. To be sure, those VCRs and TVs don't come from the United States anymore, but many of the images they transmit do. America's third largest export (after soybeans and aircraft) is entertainment. America supplies the images of the stretch limo life that keep this shell game going. So far so good, until the resources run out.

The ecotheist sees disaster ahead. Their new creed—positivism made theistic[14]—holds as a primary principle of faith that humans *can* sustain themselves indefinitely on this planet: for them, perpetuity is our mission, our destiny; this is the focus of their faith.

The skeptic, meanwhile, fundamentally challenges the ecotheist's faith. "Suppose," the skeptic might say, "that human destiny does not place us as caretakers or perpetual-care gardeners for planet Earth, as if our world were some sort of giant cemetery—endowed, changeless, and maintained in perpetuity. Suppose that human destiny is just the opposite. Suppose that we are here to process our planet, much as termites process logs fallen in the forest. Like them, our job is to render all that we are capable of consuming into a compact powder, dust, or sand."

A person holding so unfashionable a view might well point in defense to the seemingly "hard-wired" human trait of greed, the tendency of humans to extend consumption well beyond mere self-preservation into the elaborate and often dizzying heights of those cultural and personal pleasures by which we tend to measure the quality of civilizations. If the goal of human destiny were only to garden the earth in perpetuity, then why would we come so well equipped to imagine, invent, pursue, and enjoy the pleasures we are able to create beyond those required for sustenance?

The unfashionable skeptic raises a contentious but profitable question. If the ecotheist cannot account for so basic a human quality as greed, then what is our fate? But even if the skeptic is right and humans are indeed like termites, the skeptic would hasten to add: "There is no need to hurry. We have all the time in the world." And since time is a human invention, then processing the planet unto the extinction of the last human sipping a last ritual martini *is* "all the time in the world." The skeptic, here, reminds us of the forgotten quality of ritual about which both he and the ecologically faithful can agree: rituals take a lot of time. For this reason, people in a hurry absolutely hate ritual: what might be done in a matter of moments—a chalice of wine is consumed after eating a bite of bread—can drag on for hours. While this annoys the truly greedy, the termites love it: if time is all we have, then the longer anything takes the better, and the longer our consumptive destiny will continue. The irony here lies in the way ritual consumes more time than materials, in the way ritual extends time itself— that is, global human existence.

Modern ritualists often make much of the symbolic content of ritual, and some even favor adaptation of such traditional rituals as those practiced by American Indians and African peoples. These ritualists often point out the contemporary and sometimes ecological significance of these rituals' symbolic content. But from the point of view of time, the content of ritual is beside the point. If the point of ecological ritual is to prolong time—to slacken the pace of the greedy—then prolonging *pleasure* is more helpful than engaging in *symbolic meaning*.

The turn from symbolic ritual toward "pleasure-over-time" rituals then, recommends the project of the *suki* tea master: to explore the pleasure of mundane circumstances, or recalling Lao Tzu, to take *pleasure* in one's rustic tasks. Here, our skeptical termite is not unaware of the implications of action, but is circumspect about any creed or practice that would deny humans their essential quest for pleasure and satisfaction. At stake here is the interplay between *greed*, an Anglo-Saxon and largely theological term, and *pleasure*, the Latin, French, and more psychological term.

I am told that a child, given one cookie, who grabs another child's cookie as well does not necessarily exhibit greed. Placing half a cookie in each hand will prevent this "cookie aggression": the child's desire is for a cookie in each hand, and so this childhood search for pleasure achieves satisfaction without reference to absolute quantity.

For the termite, adult rituals of pleasure, such as the tea ceremonies of Japan, demonstrate a potential utility. Not in Hideyoshi's time but during the two-hundred-year-long Tokugawa shogunate that followed, Japan both languished and blossomed—a kind of hothouse in near stasis. Densely populated and at "carrying capacity," with internal political restraint preventing foreign trade or expansion, this period could be thought of as the "Tokugawa spaceship." Even so, during this time, Japanese arts flourished, creating what we have come to call "traditional Japanese design."

Among the many origins of this achievement, few can imagine it without Tea's influence. The *satisfactions* of Tokugawa life, although exercised within a virtual police state, largely derived from the tea masters' "pleasure-over-time" experiments. The results of these experiments first elevated such time-released pleasures above more ravenous indulgence and, then, demonstrated and refined the keen human satisfactions still possible within strict limitations. Although partly a function of status-quo politics, these limitations anticipated what ecological circumstances would have imposed in any case.[15]

So now, what of our own world, the stretch limo and the tenured lives it contains, striving for more than enough? What rituals of delay could nourish us? Or have the "virtual realities" of film and television made even "real time" tedious, and therefore slowed up time unbearable? What can defend ordinary reality in the face of "virtuals" of all sorts?

During chemotherapy, a late friend and colleague suggested that ecologists got the intoxicants all wrong. In laboratory tests, spiders spinning webs while on caffeine, heroin, or cocaine made a mess of it. Only the spiders spinning under the influence of cannabis managed to weave perfect webs. Their only flaw was that the webs were not finished; they were not as large as the webs spun by substance-free spiders.

The termite who wants to delay destiny might learn from the spiders.

In slow-paced societies, the focus and heightened sensitivity sometimes associated with cannabis—the conditions that allow a perfect but unfinished web—most often come through meditation, whether formally engaged or from "just sitting." Moderns who *will* meditate often achieve the same result. For them, a ritual of delay can be a real pleasure. But for those driven by hypercompetition, perhaps cannabis lacks only cultural socialization for it to be recommended.

Once upon a time, on a paradise island, as the population grew and vital species went extinct, food surpluses slowly disappeared. At a certain point, this paradise island could no longer feed the chiefs, bureaucrats, and priests who had kept its complex society running. Chaos replaced centralized government as a warrior class took control. This scenario describes not necessarily the future world inside the stretch limo, but Easter Island, where huge carved megaliths stand today as poignant relics among a severely starved people. In Japan, greater resources and a lucky combination of management and art prevented a like outcome. Europe got close, but through trade and emigration, it came to include most of the world within its food chain.

Jamaica Kincaid has written that, really, Americans are beyond greed. "A greedy person is often cross, unpleasant. Americans—at least, the ones that I am personally familiar with—are not at all cross. They are quite happy and reasonable as they take up at least twenty times as much of everything as they need." She continues, describing a house her family bought, one "at least twenty times as big as the house

This paradise island could no longer keep its complex society running
Mother of Rakaratte, the priest, Easter Island, 1911

Four orphaned children make a life for themselves in a boxcar
Gertrude Chandler Warner, *The Boxcar Children,* illustration by L. Kate Deal

I grew up in."[16] Even so, the house is not extravagant. Like American greed, the house is pleasant although, she admits, more than enough. To the world, Jamaica Kincaid lives the American dream. But where will the world go, as America exports its dreams and as the world's food chain becomes strained?

What if the stretch limo were itself to become America's "primitive hut," condensing most of the pleasures and satisfactions of American life into tiny, mobile abodes. Parked beneath a grove of trees next to a shed for our "stuff," in it we could hold our rituals of delay and our experiments with pleasure over time. On occasion, we could go places. We could pick up a "burger" and, dividing it among us, take an hour to turn fast-food into slow-food.

If the common belief is true, that we are sacrificing the rain forest for hamburgers, then what results from sanctifying this sacrifice at a snail's pace? Or, what if the stretch limo was all that we had, our primary and only abode. With stationary hookups, we could heat our stretch limo in winter, cool it in summer. With its fridge, TV, stereo sound system, and telephone/Internet, we would in many senses be "at home."

And what if we made movies about our stretch-limo life—romances, mysteries, adventures with even an occasional, ponderous chase? What would the Third World dream about then? What would be its hope? As with the cargo cults of New Guinea—who build "mock" landing fields for carriers that only land at nearby airports, disgorging what the cult believes are gifts from the Gods, intended for them—we might find Third World shanties imitating First and Second World limos, becoming long and narrow, with windshield windows and dashboard *tokonomas*. Or we might find old vehicles, permanently parked, chopped and stretched, with scrap metal or plastic between the two ends. What if the dream of our stretch limo life caught on all around the termites' world: might we gradually see a world of tiny abodes of modest convenience and comfort, prolonging, for as long as possible, pleasures we have come to value but pleasures we might all share? Perhaps the idea is absurd and ridiculous. And well it might be. It is, after all, only a movie.

Or is it? Ask the homeless who now live out of their vehicles. If the average American lives only three paychecks from such homelessness, then experiments like that of the stretch limo already surround us. From one point of view this is, of course, a tragedy. But tragic, too, is a world that cannot sustain us all.

Making *Believe*

Until Humpty-Dumpty falls from a wall of *concrete*—not of brick or stone—there can be no dependable clientele for modern architecture. Until Little Red Riding Hood's grandmother lives in a cottage modeled after the Barcelona Pavilion, the appeal of childhood literature will instead sustain a domestic market for pitched roofs and mullioned windows. It may be just that simple.

Even nowadays, simple stories and their illustrations require a child's appetite for enchantment and imagination. More specifically, classic adventure stories, like *Robinson Crusoe* and *Treasure Island*, help ground this satisfaction in the real world, where fictitious forts and shelters likely bridge our earliest encounter to the primitive hut, even before we build our own.

Less familiar may be the story of *The Boxcar Children*. In the world on their own, four orphaned children—by their own effort, skill, and wit—make a life for themselves in a boxcar they find abandoned in some woods. Those who remember this story may recall the thrill and satisfaction we imagined should we, too, fulfill all our needs by ourselves. But *The Boxcar Children* gives such satisfaction a special twist. Bracketing their life in the boxcar is a grandfather the orphans fear would be mean should they fall under his care. Instead, he materializes as a kindly benefactor who overcomes their suspicions, takes them into his household, and eventually installs the boxcar (along with its entrance stump and domestic objects) in one of his gardens. As the author says of this reunion, "The children ran over to it with cries of delight. . . . All the things were in place. . . . Here was the old knife which had cut butter and bread and vegetables and firewood and string. Here was Benny's pink cup, and here was his bed. Here were the big kettle and blue tablecloth. Here were the pitcher and the old teapot."[17]

"But," as a grown-up friend of mine said of the transplanted boxcar, "it won't be the same." Just as jousting was not the same as medieval combat and the tea ritual is not the same as a mountain reclusion, the children's encounters with the transplanted boxcar will become the surrogate of a past life, if they happen at all.

But for the occasional homesteader, no one fulfills all their own needs directly anymore. Instead, surrogate activities abound in contemporary life—from fishing to gardening, from off-road vehicle contests to mock war games.

Perhaps the twentieth-century grand master of surrogate activity is Marcel Duchamp. Among the "affluent, idle, or privileged—as an ostensibly lazy and amused chess-playing bachelor dilettante," Duchamp and his circle shared interests in numerology, mythic and erotic symbols, and linguistic ciphers.[18] These sources provide the allusions that, for them, became—like chess—both a game and a kind of work. As grown children in an immense boxcar of marginal utility, the group's members played a "vibrant ancient magical game plumbing the wisdom, nonsense, and proliferating meanings inherent in language, images, sounds, and accidents of association."[19]

Perhaps Duchamp's best-known piece, the *Fountain*—a urinal turned upside down and inscribed, "R. Mutt 1917"—was actually a collaboration of discovery, modification, submission (to the New York Society of Independent Artists), suppression, retrieval, and subsequent publication and photograph dissemination involving Man Ray, Pierre Roché, Beatrice Woods, Alfred Stieglitz, Marsden Hartley, and Duchamp's friend, collaborator, and patron Walter Arensberg.

Visitors who crowd museums to view this and other Duchamp masterpieces largely mistake the evidence for the action, the guard signal for the train. Absent in the museum is any sense of the intense play of their inception. In the gallery, where the viewer's eye, disembodied, looks to attach itself to meaning or enchantment, Duchamp's objects give away very little. Each piece forms less an art object than the final stage in a "bored"-game, whose rules and codes are largely unknown except to its players.

But in a world that has learned to mistake shock for revelation, Duchamp's success has all but obliterated his larger lesson: "Do as I do." That is, the satisfaction of such surrogate activities as his lies in their play rather than their products, in engagement rather than the disembodied eye, as if Duchamp is saying, "Seek satisfaction in your own play." At best, the disembodied eye can be amused or entranced, but—as with sports activities—the satisfaction of accomplishment belongs to the players, not to the spectators.

Our world is not the same as Duchamp's. Our disembodied eye seeks satisfactions far less from the White Cube of the gallery and far more from the Black Cube of film and television. Here, the eye glazes as if in a dream state and disembodiment is nearly complete. Here images and stories are not obscure; they are clear and paramount—the very object that film presents. Film gives us stories with meanings and morals. In this sense film may be akin to salon paintings, what Duchamp called "retinal art." While salon paintings appear as flash frames where tableaux freeze both stories and figures, suggesting both meaning and moral, film defrosts and sets them in motion.

While seemingly benign, film's disembodiment joins it to other mass media to form what Guy Debord calls *spectacle*, wherein "[e]verything that was directly lived has moved away into a representation."[20] As a surrogate activity to replace tasks of necessity with tasks of play, spectacle no more satisfies us—however it may amuse or instruct—than any other spectator sport. Mass media is not necessity's surrogate, but its escape.

News commentator Roger Rosenblatt recently identified one of the most perplexing issues of our time: "How," he asked, "do we regain our experience in a world of mass culture?" How, indeed, do we regain a world that is *directly lived*, as it was for the Chinese recluses and the desert fathers, or as it is now for some of today's homeless.

Michael Benedikt has argued that real as opposed to media experiences can be profoundly moving: "Precisely from such moments . . . we build our best and necessary sense of an independent yet meaningful reality. I should like to call them *direct esthetic experiences of the real.*"[21] But where Benedikt argues that it falls to architecture to offer this experience, I offer instead the hut and its rituals. Even if such huts and rituals are merely a world of "make-believe," as Kenzo Tange has suggested, all the same they are "an emotionally satisfying little world."[22] Moreover, whether in the teahouse to which Tange alludes, or the *casita*, the boxcar, the folly, or the *hameau*, "make-believe" becomes real because *it is made.*

Tucked into the margins of many northern European cities, one can find allotment parks provided by statutory agreement for its citizens to use. Typically, an array of allotment plots is fenced off from the surrounding area; each plot in turn is fenced from the others. Footpaths or narrow lanes connect the plots, which form a kind of neighborhood in miniature and in season. In an established allotment park, we might find a few mature trees, hedges, and small groves. Most people use these plots for gardening, but often these plots will contain a small shed where, "behind a barrier of beans, [one can] read the paper and smoke and be away from home without self-reproach."[23]

Other allotment parks, with common toilet and bathing facilities, permit habitable huts or tiny cottages. Here a gate may open onto a formal gravel path that leads through a clipped lawn, rose borders, and statuary to a tiny dwelling. We can only guess the make-believe games of their owners by the clues we read from their settings: some are symmetrically arranged tiny villas, others are more casual cabins. Whatever the intention, these are all physically made places, with all the necessary tasks attendant thereto: sweeping the path, clearing the gutters, patching the windows, pruning

In enclaves of make-believe, the isolated hut turns social
Allotment Park near Copenhagen, 1967

the shrubs. And they exist in a real world with its own habits and tasks that we call *seasons*—those real, in-the-world experiences that mass media has demoted into holidays with greeting cards and presents.

I can imagine figures like Sue spending time here, cooking up strange or plain dishes. In enclaves of make-believe, the isolated primitive hut, once associated with reclusion, real or ornamental, turns social. Through ritual play, participants achieve the satisfaction of make-believe grounded in the real world and in each other. In the process, these enclaves also expand the traditional role of surrogate activity; they keep up the skills and the sensibilities of a soon-to-be-extinct generation, should anyone ever need these skills and sensibilities again.

The satisfactions of this make-believe world may not turn the world around, but it can radically alter our own position in the world. In a world of media surrogates, *making* believe may be all we have. Even so, it might be enough.

Interval

The Hut as Gallery

Jodie Foster's camera crew filmed an empty rotunda. Not even a ghost of the hut remained; it had already been reborn, elsewhere, in the open air. And by the time *Little Man Tate*, hutless, had garnered generally positive reviews—"Two thumbs up!" said Siskel and Ebert—I had begun building another hut. This would be a different sort of hut—*much* different.

It began as a colonnade, fifty feet long, its columns, two feet apart, lengthwise, and three feet apart, widthwise. This double row of columns—what architects sometimes call a datum, the basic move that organizes all ensuing moves—could be extended in one direction, all the way to the street, while in the opposing direction, a dense grove of trees and the property line blocked further expansion.

Working with a former student named Tim, I set out to enclose parts of this datum using the method I had employed in the first hut: we made mock-ups of each temporary decision, tested its results, and then cut plywood panels or cedar flaps to fit around every window sash, once we established its placement.

When I sat in this narrow slice of space, at its dead end, I thought about the questions I had yet to ask. In the first two huts—really the same hut in two locations—I had discovered the magic of the hearth and its performances, but I had yet to explore the hearth's traditional partner, the *tokonoma*.

In the first two huts, the *tokonoma* was merely a side alcove, with only a supporting role. But in teahouses, *tokonomas* function the same way that mantelpieces do on Western fireplaces—except that Western mantels more or less permanently display their owners' most iconic, nostalgic objects, while, in teahouses the *tokonoma's* contents change with each use. Thus, I reasoned, if the hearth suggested that the teahouse was like a diminutive theater, then the *tokonoma* suggested that it was also like an intimate gallery, one for temporary exhibits.

The saloon-gallery began as a double row of columns, fifty feet long

A third row of columns accommodates the back bar

The words *intimate gallery* called up a distant memory, a flashback. It is now some years earlier; I have just sketched an idea for a tiny roadside saloon. Along a backcountry road sits a modest structure with a boomtown front and a front porch to scale. Inside rests a bar without stools, because the floor rises to just an inch or two below the top of the counter. And behind the bar, in the space where bottles usually advertise themselves, I imagined an alcove, painted white like a gallery—so like a gallery that my imagination hung a painting or two in it.

I had shown my sketch to a painter friend. He said it was like being in a gallery where you could do what you always want to in a gallery: you could sit down. "If I knew people were going to actually sit and look at my work," he said, "it might change everything I do. It might change art entirely."

I began to think of all the other things that might change art entirely: the challenges to modern aestheticism and the gallery's antiritual, the taste for uncanniness and concerns for ecology among today's gallerygoers, the call for a new vision beyond the binding forms of freedom. I thought of the starveling formalist man seeking nourishment and satisfaction. From my seat at the dead end of my narrow space, I wondered if my experiments there might somehow find a way out.

Recalling my sketch, I saw in it a pair of new metaphors: the hut as saloon, the hut as gallery. Then, it occurred to me that the two metaphors were really the same: the word *saloon* being a corruption of the French *salon*—a living room of high society, and also the use of such rooms for collecting Parisian intellectuals or for exhibiting art, as in the *Salon des Refusés* or the *Salon des Indépendants*.

Catherine the Great's Hermitage—originally a small *salon* for her art collection that grew into a huge museum—also connoted reclusion of a sort: a diminutive space set apart from daily life, a cabinet for curiosity, a little house for pleasure. Similarly, in English, and later in American parlance, the *salon* or the saloon-bar was less a place for art and intellect than for convivial conversation.

A metaphor this rich in meaning and reference can suggest many directions, leading to all sorts of typically American spaces, from juke joints to diners. Yet any one of these inspirations, if too strictly referenced, would preclude others.

For now, though, my long and narrow space was sufficiently abstract as to accept all these metaphorical cousins. All it lacked was a bar, and of course, a back bar. So, with the help of another former student, Wenyi, I set a third row of framing posts parallel to the first two. We enclosed part of the space thus defined as a place for the host to stand in front of the back bar. Here, the host could look straight into the eyes of customers or guests, the way bartenders normally do, and these guests could gaze, seated on the floor, straight into the eyes of art.

Ah, but what sort of art could dare to meet that intimate gaze? What art could redefine itself so as to be at home in this new gallery? If the concept of "inhabitation by ritual" had guided the experiments in my first hut, then perhaps "inhabitation by exhibition" might suggest those in my newest one.

For my trial run as an art entrepreneur, I chose five small etchings by Jan Volf and wrote bits of commentary that updated a classic Grimm's fairy tale. Wonderfully grotesque, each etching was a wry, little commentary in its own right. When put together with the tale of an old couple living in a hovel—who catch a magic fish and whose escalating greed bring them, in my version, from hovel to ranch house to Homerama Home to Park Avenue penthouse and back to their original hovel again—the result was chilling. Everyone being acutely conscious that the structure in which they were sitting was itself little better than a hovel gave the cautionary tale an almost painful physicality. All five guests took turns reading parts of the story and, unlike standard gallery practice, we handed around the etchings as the story unfolded. Afterwards, one guest packed in the middle of the other four grinned: "This has been so uncomfortable that it *was* comfortable."

After this qualified triumph, I tested the consequences of giving guests artwork to hold. If you could hold the work, you could also turn it over and so there might be a back side, not on public display, for semiprivate viewing. I asked the class of a colleague, Gail Della Piana, to make up some images for the gallery hut that took advantage of this double-faced display. Because this exhibition occurred soon after the Mapplethorpe brouhaha just down the road in Cincinnati, I imagined that some students might discover the secret of displaying images others might find "pornographic." But rather than hiding indecencies, these students more often hid personal memories and sentiments—modern indecencies of another sort. Breaking taboos of content, we had violated the accustomed sanctity of the gallery wall and of gallery deportment as well. Like Toto in the Kingdom of Oz, we had peeked behind the curtain.

For the gallery's third exhibition, I invited Seymour Howard to be both artist and host. Because he enjoys coaxing his viewers into wordplay with his images, I thought this gallery might suit him—and my experiment. His work—ideograms, he calls them—function like Rorschach blots and can have many possible interpretations: archetypal, geometric, Freudian, and Jungian. A few guests played along:

"It looks like a fish."

"Yes, good: fish, Pisces, π-seas, pie sees, a seeing pie. Go on . . ."

"Well, I guess it also looks like a woman, kind of buxom—a mother figure."

"A mother's pie, mother, *mater*, matter, does it matter?"

This improvisational wordplay continued as ridiculous and profound meanings tumbled out, willy-nilly. Gallery or not, this half-empty/half-full space had actively engaged these "viewers." No longer spectators, we were Duchampian playmates.

For the fourth exhibition, I persuaded a painter, Terry Barrett, to completely line the hut's interior with paintings: to sheathe the back bar's three sides and cover the wall behind the guests. I also asked her to include as many images of people as possible, so that we might sense all of art history

At its dead end, I thought about the questions I had yet to ask

surrounding us—perhaps, I imagined, bidding us farewell. She made large figures of women and wolves' heads, tiny images of maybe-kings or heroes, and one haunting face I thought so enigmatically and profoundly blank, I could only imagine it as a figure who saw things just as they were— staring back at us. For this exhibit, I adapted cappuccino-making to a ritual, to see what effect performance might add to this gallerylike experience. After the ritual had drifted into a particularly intense conversation, one guest said, "Has anyone here ever read *The Book of Tea*? I don't know why, but this has all reminded me a bit of Okakura."

Bingo! I'd been waiting years to hear a stranger say something like that.

On a recent trip to California, I decided to revisit my first tea hut, in the backyard of a house sold long ago and ever after rented. When the current tenant took me around to the back, I found a heap of lumber where the tea hut once stood.

"It was falling apart," the tenant explained. "Then a big wind came along and took it all down."

I made inquiries and learned that, among various tenants, the tea hut had served as a child's playhouse but more often as a storage shed. Neither the owner nor any of his tenants had thought to reroof or repair it. Instead, the hut lingered on as a pile of familiar debris. I picked up a few boards and panels and reassembled the hut around them in my memory.

"I'm sure you can keep any of it you want," the tenant said.

A former neighbor helped me sort through the remains. "It might make an interesting partial reconstruction," we told each other as a neat, deliberate pile rose beside the chaotic one. Out of the blue—perhaps to distract me from a wallow in nostalgia—he said: "I think you should meet Jimi Suzuki."

Jimi lived nearby, along a street of modest suburban houses, in one that looked pretty much like the rest. But inside teemed a treasure trove, a giant cabinet of curiosity. Every room was stuffed with oddities, rarities, delicacies,

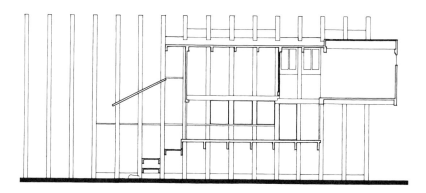

All of art history surrounded us, perhaps bidding farewell

and ephemera. A lamp, whose exposed bulb held a tiny filament in the shape of an elephant, glowed with a greenish light when Jimi turned it on. Bell jars held Jimi's constructions of images and objects: postcards, butterflies, dolls' heads, dice, tiny figurines, and toys. Wherever one looked, one saw collections of shells, broken teacups, chess sets, pottery plates and vases, stacks of books, pictures, and photo albums. On the wall, his tiny collages turned this three-dimensional bazaar into two-dimensional vignettes, juxtaposing the classic and the casual, the sacred and the strange.

Jimi is an artist from Tokyo. "I come here to hide," he said.

But his reclusion here is active and arresting, his art influenced by Duchamp. His puns and play find humor, irony, and meaning in things most of us don't even see. I asked him about a collection of wine bottles along the window of his studio. They no longer contained wine, but odd bits of paper and small objects instead. Each cork had something else affixed to it too: feathers, twisted metal, tiny heads, or toy birds.

"Oh, those," Jimi said. "Sometimes when we finish a bottle, we put things back inside. It's kind of a joke, sometimes. But not always. Here is one from my daughter's twenty-first birthday. Look, I made a new label for it."

I left Jimi's house fairly bursting with ideas. I began to picture where the wine bottles might go in *my* little gallery. I imagined allotment huts where neighbors might build memories from rituals like Jimi's. My mind raced.

Still, I couldn't help recalling the hut that had once stood in my backyard. As interesting as my experiments with gallery life had been, they somehow lacked the magic that I remembered from the first hut. While this may have been nostalgia, as my neighbor suspected, perhaps it was not *only* nostalgia.

Architects in Transition

four

Taken for Granted

As we are born into air, we are born into buildings. After that, we tend to take both for granted. The frailty of our human bodies and the advantage of our opposable thumbs make buildings so necessary and possible that they don't seem artifical at all. Instead, they seem an extension of the earth's circumstance and our own being in the world.

Consequently, as we walk through our lives, day by day, architecture and building *is* the landscape, the terrain, the atmosphere in which we move. Most of the time, we do not really want it any other way. Our conscious awareness focuses far less on our surroundings than on our major preoccupations: am I successful? am I loved? Or on minor ones: does the bank close at 5 or 6 o'clock on Fridays? Despite architects' efforts to get our attention, we quickly subordinate buildings to these more personal concerns.

When I was a kid and adults said "taken for granted," I heard instead, "taken for granite." In most contexts, a curious phrase; in some, quite powerful: "You are taking me for granite" (stony face, and all).

Many recent buildings, called "postmodern," are precisely intended to be taken for granite, as if they were literally written in stone. Even so, they are made of steel and the other constituents of today's modern building "species"— a species equally dependent on tempered glass, asphalt-membrane roofing, neoprene gaskets, hydraulic elevators— not to mention the necessary network of construction skills, transportation options, labor agreements, and capital investments that they require. But though we take these buildings for granted, nothing guarantees their perpetuity. As a species, modern buildings may one day be extinct. Even Walter Gropius's 1938 house can't be completely restored; no one manufactures its linoleum flooring anymore.

Today, our "granite" buildings sport a wallpaper of stone, cut to resemble solid load-bearing blocks. But, if you bump into one, it rings hollow; if you put your hand on one, it does not feel cold. Its little punched windows imply solidity, but from their shallow sills, you easily detect the deception. This is not a solid building; this is a cartoon of a solid building, a cartoon in the Renaissance sense—a drawing or model that creates a proposal at full scale. Occasionally, too, such buildings are also cartoons in the twentieth-century meaning.

What is the purpose of such cartooning? If we take a cartoon building and lift its stone cladding, we find, to no one's surprise, a modern building. Beginning in the 1970s, we have come to read such undecorated modern buildings as stark, sterile, cold and, worst of all, boring and uncelebrating. Now, we project new desires onto the very buildings that only a generation earlier we admired for their purity (now read, *starkness*) and serenity (now read, *boredom*).

But how can we account for these new projections? The most immediate answer may lie in a special historic circumstance—one that may also demonstrate how architecture works culturally. Historically, this about-face—which exposes both modern and "postmodern" architecture—begins in the postwar world of opportunity when success came relatively easily. Businessmen made fortunes in new products for a booming economy; professors got tenure without asking for it. All the while, unadorned modern buildings celebrated the ease and casualness of postwar success.

Things began to get dicey, and turned around when the economy slowed several times in the 1970s and the mid 1980s. Coincidentally, the baby boomers entered the scene and found, to their surprise, they were not alone. For every success dream, hundreds stood in line. Even when the economy picked up in the late 1980s, all found the world in which they lived was no longer casual. They now lived in a world of hypercompetition where *success and survival* had become much the same thing. Moreover, in this world of hypercompetition, the purity and serenity of modernism no longer appeared helpful.

In the game of hypercompetition, one can win through bluffs, lies, and pretenses. In the world we take for granted, and for granite, the key strategy is the lie. The commercial lie tells others that not only is this company, firm, or individual successful, but equally important, it has been successful *for a long time*. What else explains the cold-blooded architectural references to English gentlemen's-club interiors, with wood-paneled wainscot, hunt-scene prints, and the like? Similarly, suburbia tells a corresponding domestic lie: that this couple, this family comes from a successful past and has a promising future—no divorce, no bankruptcy here.

If these buildings don't seem to bother anyone, it is because architecture is not their primary concern. In fact, both the commercial and domestic worlds prefer to take the message of these images for granted. The success we exhibit is not provisional, not ironic, not temporary, not unstable. We live in a cartoon landscape that supports our desires for success and love in times when these are scarce, restricted, regulated, protected. We believe one another's lies because our own lie depends on it.

This new architecture, called "postmodern," is only the new species of buildings we wish to take for granted. Notwithstanding the current pullulation of coffee-table books, the possibility for architecture is slim these days. This slim possibility, then, lies in the occasional way that building may allow some direct brush with the underlying emotions of success (the sublime, perhaps) or the emotions of love (the intimate, maybe). But who might build these sublime or intimate places, and why? Perhaps someone in the margins of architecture, beneath the shelter of the primitive hut. In societies like ours, where architecture and history *make* meaning out of vast and shifting complexities, the primitive hut is a search and an attempt to pare away what is given and apparent, to find something else to satisfy our deepest emotions. What is timeless in the primitive huts of societies with history and architecture is precisely this search.

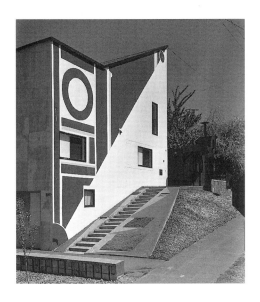

We have come to read unclad buildings as boring and uncelebrating
The Humana Building and the First National Tower, Louisville, c. 1990

Treehouses and playhouses are the genesis of the contemporary primitive hut
Treehouse, Oxford, Ohio, 1997

Few people saw Rob Reichert's target. Nice people would curse
Reichert House, Seattle, 1952, photo by Charles A. Pearson

Venturi's talent was getting us to see the target he saw
Vanna Venturi House, Robert Venturi, Philadelphia, 1963

In previous centuries, this search answered the agenda of its time. In our own time, Joseph Rykwert made two stunning contributions to its present-day position: he reidentified the broad genre we know as the primitive hut and he insisted upon its *universal* significance as "a reminder of the original and therefore essential meaning of all building for people."[1] Deconstructionists now find his appeal to the "universal," "original" and "essential" fodder for dispute. But when Rykwert's book first appeared—two decades ago, in a cultural and economic climate of larger and more bombastic buildings—the very idea of attending at all to modest, sometimes rustic structures was entirely remarkable.

But while Rykwert saw the primitive hut as a universal artifact, the product of a "haunting" vision and a "collective memory kept alive . . . by legends and rituals,"[2] Gaston Bachelard added a more phenomenological interpretation of the hut vision and its "unfathomable oneiric depth."[3] While Rykwert's primitive is founded in the expression of origins—collectively imagined and believed, Bachelard's primitive is founded in the expressions of youth, not as vulgar nostalgia (as he emphatically warns), but in "images as we should have imagined them during the 'original impulse' of youth." These primal images "give us back . . . houses in which the human being's certainty of being is concentrated, and we have the impression that . . . in images that are as stabilizing as these are, we could start a new life, a life that would be our own, that would belong to us in our very depths."[4]

It would seem, then, that the search for the primitive hut begins in play, a deconstructing process in which children seem to examine what is given them, intent upon taking it apart. Such searches bring some children to build, or simulate forts, treehouses, clubhouses, playhouses, and, more recently, rocket ships. These are the universal genesis of primitive huts in cultures with architecture and history. These experiences lead children to alternative views of the world, so that one day they may gaze upon their parents' attachments as the blind sentiments of a soon-to-be-extinct species. Like a game of leapfrog, just as one generation has hoisted itself over the backs of its parents, the next generation begins its own leap over them.

By playing "house" or "fort," children actually mimic the processes of architecture. From the props at hand, they imagine alternative scenarios and anticipate a variety of unseen participants. Like designers, they obsess over details that seem meaningless to others. Despite meager prompting, both children and architects conjure worlds as yet unseen.

What Architecture Is

Space aliens who monitor our news might imagine that architects run things here on Earth: "'So and so' was the architect of the buyout," they hear. And another "so and so" was "the architect of the peace accord." To the space alien, architects seem to do the things that matter most on Earth.

Should our observers' curiosity ever lead them to the schools that train these architects, they might anticipate lectures about finance or diplomacy. Instead, our space aliens encounter talk about *space*! In one classroom, they hear of "space frames"; in another, "defensible space"; in a third, "modern vs. 'postmodern' space."

"Ah yes," they might recall. "Werner Von Braun, architect of the *space* program." To the space alien, there seems to be nothing that architects don't do.

For this reason, it may surprise our space alien that earthlings' dictionaries connect architects with the construction of buildings.

"Buildings?" they might wonder. "There are never any buildings in the news."

If space aliens write memoirs, then those who observed us in the eighteenth century would have given a much different account. Then, kings made peace, princes made deals, and architecture was making the news. Architects built bridges to span impassable rivers and fortifications to defend whole towns, they built palaces to refine aristocratic sensibilities and boulevards to refine urban behavior. The architect had his ear to the ground and his eye to the future. Fearless of failure, he designed bridges that collapsed, fortifications that were breached. Eventually failure made theory and theory made experts—today's engineers. This left the architect back with the palaces and the boulevards, with sensibilities and behavior.

As the architects of buildings no longer made the news, their quarrels became heated because the stakes were so small. No one but architects cared so passionately about the orders and proportion, nature and beauty. Not until the invention of genius.

As the Enlightenment's house pet, the genius possessed imagination, originality, and creativity. If "talent is like the marksman who hits a target which others cannot reach; genius is like the marksman who hits a target . . . which others cannot even see."[5]

While the eighteenth century fixed its sights on the order inherent in nature as created by God, some would try to hit this target by rational means—formal and mathematical. Others would try empirically, by observation and experiment. But, in the nineteenth century, neither patrons nor God would tether the genius. He would become secular democracy's hero. Buoyed now by popular support, the genius could push God and kings aside.

To the degree that architecture was still a "heaping together of parts," these constructions no longer sought out God's order in the universe but an order that would please Man. The fickleness of democracy's understanding and appreciation isolated the genius, who created "out of nothing, as God had supposedly done, or at the very least out of his own soul."[6] In return, the public heaped the rewards of fame, but only upon those persons of genius who hit the targets that the public could be persuaded they could see.

While the genius risks isolation, futility, and perhaps madness as well, the myth of genius accounts for some future time when others come to see the target the genius sees, or as Richard Rorty has suggested, to have use for it. Rorty argues that this happy confluence would be contingent, not upon some absolute achievement but rather upon historical circumstances, "some particular need that a given community happens to have at a given time. . . . [and] results from the accidental coincidence of a private obsession with a public need."[7]

Genius architects are rare; the cost of building precludes targets that clients can't at least imagine. Even so, one genius architect comes to mind, one who—as is often said of genius—was ahead of his time. In the early 1950s, Bob Reichert built a few houses, all starkly modern and painted white, with bold, black abstract patterns. The exterior of Reichert's own house, in 1952, combined modern strip windows with the enlarged painted shadow pattern of Santa Maria del Fiore. It was his best work, and also the most controversial. "I was breaking fresh ice. Thick ice. I paid for it. People would dump garbage on my driveway. Nice people would curse."[8] Few saw Reichert's target until Robert Venturi awakened in us a need for historic reference or named and demonstrated the "decorated shed"; not until *Complexity and Contradiction* made Robert Venturi and his work famous could we see Bob Reichert's target, or our own need for it.

While Reichert had genius, Venturi possessed talent. Venturi got us to see the target he saw: an architecture combining modernist and historic sensibilities, an architecture that "evokes many levels of meaning and combinations of *focus . . . readable* and workable in several ways at once."[9] Reichert may have embraced this target first, but to Venturi has gone the fame that results from the desires we could not see, the desires he anticipated, named and awakened.

Such architects of talent work by design, crafting schemes with preconceived and well-communicated ends. Their work is full of affect. They tease and fulfill our major or minor preoccupations by material means. They work by evocative seduction and prurient subterfuge. And not incidentally, the fame of the architect transfers with no loss to his or her client.

But how could architecture and design have come so far from the promises of modernism: the worship of utility, function, and mass production? Or from Le Corbusier's famous dictum: "The house is a machine for living in."[10] In likening the design of buildings to the design of machines, how could the modern designer forget that the production of machines includes the not incidental participation of industrialists who concern themselves less with utility or function than with marketing and sales.

Consider the VCR. Internally all are essentially the same. Only when these nearly identical machines are encased in a variety of shells can they be differentiated by the consumer. This step—between manufacture and distribution—the modernists virtually ignored but, today, as this step becomes exaggerated and professionalized, it defines the condition of design in our time.

But superficial differentiation through design may not really be the rupture that modernists think. Le Corbusier's manifesto reveals the seeds not only of functionalism but of stylism as well; he calls for "all the animation that the artist's sensibility can add to severe and pure functioning elements."[11] And what is this sensibility but *differentiation*, demanded as much by the consumer as by the industrialist, a kind of endless dance of desires raised, differentiated, and fulfilled, over and over again: the differentiation that gives bragging rights, whether at the level of houses and teakettles or at the level of blue jeans and cologne.

Still, there are a few archetypal architects—those who approach a project as if it were a totally new VCR, guts and all. Their occasional achievement reminds us how much most architects miss. About a recent Tokyo building by Raphael Viñoly, Herbert Merscahamp writes:

> It is almost unheard of for architects today to devote themselves to this level of detail. We pretend not to mind, because if we did we'd go crazy. We accept that architects develop concepts, sketches, drawings and models, and then hand the project over to an "associated" firm to create the physical object in space. Here we're dealing with a radically different economy of mind. The bolt beneath our feet emerged from the

same esthetic intelligence that conceived the space around it. An architect is making architecture, and we almost can't stand it. It is dizzying to realize that excellence is a polite term for obsession.[12]

Today, in architecture offices all over the world, young men and women engage tasks that seldom come close to such obsession. Bottom-line office economics discourage it. Hunched over CAD terminals, these designers try to differentiate not so much between the extraordinary and the unremarkable, but between the building at hand and the office's last one. They are stylists of the large gesture, the details of which are too costly to explore.

Still, the myth of total architecture is alive in the schools. As students, today's designers were inspired and trained to do more than they are ever asked to. For many of these students what architecture is is a big disappointment.

What Architecture Isn't

In the last scene of the movie *Smoke*, Harvey Keitel and William Hurt share a table in a New York delicatessen. Behind Keitel we see glass deli cases; behind Hurt we see shelves of cans and packages. While Keitel tells his story, we have time to examine the venue in some detail.

Eventually we see the table itself: ribbed chrome strips edge a Formica-like top, the sort of table you'd associate with dinette sets of the 1950s. Both the table and the deli appear unremarkable. We've seen ones like them before and we sense, falsely, that we can see them again, anytime. The setting is ordinary, the accumulation of years of inattention to the whole but with intermittent attention to posters posted, signs inserted, calendars hung and replaced. These places give the impression of being undesigned; they appear to have generated themselves; they are places everyone takes for granted. Even so, they are endangered.

Those that do exist are less a tribute to our attention than to city building codes that unwittingly aid and abet such preservation. By requiring complete but costly updates, should their owners make even modest improvements, these codes—despite the pressures for new and trendy change—assure that some places like these will remain untouched. Those that do survive often become meccas for people who tire of the designers' tease. They allow us, like Keitel and Hurt, to tell our stories undistracted.

We often say of these undesigned places that they possess *authenticity;* they are the genuine article. After years of routine maintenance, they remain the very same places—with the same counters, stools, mirrors, and walls—we may recall from childhood, or imagine from a time past. But their appeal is not always nostalgic. Nostalgia arises from designs that date themselves. Places that evoke nostalgia were designed to be "in style" once and have now gone out. Authentic places had little overt style in the first place. What appeals in authenticity is designer neglect: the absence of style intended to ingratiate, to excite, or to dazzle—to differentiate. Like old-growth forests, authentic places preserve the machinations of microprocesses that are still occurring.

Even new places can achieve authenticity when the pretense behind their creation is weak. Often these places draw our attention more to their longing than to their achievement.

I recall a fishing contest in Chrisfield, a tidewater town in Maryland. Along a ramshackle wooden pier, someone had strung a few lights, some faded pennants, and a pathetically small banner. A designer might have made a big deal of this, but instead, the scene conveyed a feeble gaiety, a poignant bravery. And these tentative gestures marked an event not even present; the fishing parties sat in boats somewhere out on the water, too far to be seen.

For this reason, the banners and pennants resemble the rope and paper *shimenawa* that mark many Shinto sites. Waving in the breeze, they promise that something unseen will eventually make itself present. And similarly, the modest pier resembled the Omiwa shrine, an inconsequential structure that shelters visitors who worship three rocks they cannot actually see, but where they believe the *kami* (spirits) dwell. In each case, invisible expectation makes a dead-flat reality into a sacred precinct. The first boat, as it emerges— a smudge on the horizon at dusk—becomes a moment of *utsuroi*, when the *kami* spirits are believed to first enter and occupy a vacant space.

But how does this minimalist provision for the unseen square with architecture's long tradition of sacred space? Could it be that the god we recognize in the sacred space of architecture is really Architecture itself, or more specifically now, after the invention of genius, the architect's completed achievement—by design, calculation, and intention?

Every year, schools of architecture graduate more students than there are architects in practice. These graduates then go from an academy that cares only about architecture's ideals into a world that cares about them very little. Like acolytes, these students have learned the faith of the priests who taught them. They have learned to divide the world into what is real (what is seen) and what is not real (the unseen). Beyond this basic binary dualism lie others, dividing the faithful into schisms that make the radical Reformation in Germany— where minute differences of dogma divided and redivided towns and villages—seem ecumenical by comparison.

But beyond their divisions, the faithful are united in their collective—although masked—*ressentiment*. Born of a will to power, a will to build, a will for fame, this resentment comes from the fact that architects, although they are relentlessly trained to do so, do not make our world and only very few of them ever make the news. For this reason, perhaps no one appreciates places like delicatessens, diners, and fishing festivals more than architects do. For us, these places reveal a bracing heresy—that something else is a truer, more noble object of worship than Architecture itself. This heresy staggers us; we feel incapable of *ever* designing for this sensibility.

In a sense, like James Agee, we hold a "thief's right" to such realms. Writing about a crude sharecropper's house in Alabama, Agee not only perceives the beauty of the seen but of the unseen as well:

Not many places preserve the impression of being undesigned
Glen Miller's Diner, 1979, photo by Elliott Kauffman

Rope and paper shiminawa *promise that something unseen will eventually be present*
Okutsu-iwakura, Omiwa Shrine, Japan

". . . one among the serene and final, incomparable beauties of existence"
Sharecroppers' house, Alabama, 1941, photo by Walker Evans

"It is exercising for me. This is something important, for myself"
Guineo's house, photo © Margaret Morton and Diana Balmori, *Transitory Gardens, Uprooted Lives,* Yale University Press, 1993

[this] house of simple people which stands empty and silent in the vast Southern country morning sunlight, . . . [is], not to me but of itself, one among the serene and final, uncapturable beauties of existence: . . . this beauty is made between hurt and invincible nature and the plainest cruelties and needs of human existence in this uncured time. And is inextricable among these, and as impossible without them as a saint born in paradise.[13]

Unseen here—in the hurt and needs of human existence—is the pattern of relentless labor barely rewarded, of achievement never recognized, of sacrifice routinely expected—in short, the nature of human existence as many people experience it, unadorned by civilization's confections and most certainly untouched by architecture's joie de vivre.

The practitioners of the Japanese tea ceremony borrowed the term *wabi* to describe the essence of their pursuit. Roughly translated, *wabi* meant poverty, or "not to be in the fashionable society of the time. . . . to be satisfied with a little hut, like the log cabin of Thoreau, and with a dish of vegetables picked in the neighboring fields."

However, as D. T. Suzuki pointed out, should a person be unable to abide the insufficiency of his condition, then "he would no more be a man of *wabi* but a poverty-stricken person."[14] But what draws Agee and the tea practitioners to rustic poverty in the first place? Is their attraction merely a pose of cultural sophistication?

I would have thought so but for a child's voice overheard coming from a playhouse next door. Apparently several children were gearing up for some childhood charade, for which one child was being sent indoors to get props. The call of a slightly older child cleared my fence for me to hear and ponder for years: "Don't forget . . . We're *very* poor."

What imaginings did this call evince? Could it be that these children imagined themselves the inhabitants of a primitive hut, there to experience the shiver of needs only

barely fulfilled? Did these children manifest a vague antici-
pation of possibility and make of their play a strategy of cop-
ing, of maintaining an attitude amicable with life?

Or is this impulse even more basic—not merely contingent upon the vagaries of twentieth-century uncertainty? Is
it possible that what I had overheard derived from a hard-
wired impulse to revisit the basic contract of human survival—an impulse so deep that it had compelled Agee to appreciate even those who had not taken to rustic poverty
voluntarily?

A Hut of One's Own

Today's hut dwellers inhabit the margins of every American
city. The lucky ones live in shacks cobbled together from
odd pieces of wood and metal, plastic and cardboard. I call
them "lucky" because most cities prefer these people in
"shelters" of some sort, sleeping on cots all in a row, their
meals and rest periods fixed and strictly enforced. Consequently, those who've managed to build a hut of their own
will fear—superseding all the fears projected by others on
their behalf—discovery, eviction, and a life among the cots
all in a row.

There are reasons, of course, why reasonable societies
discourage such enterprise. To rid Paris of the tramps' and
vagabonds' romantic existence under the bridges of the
Seine, Le Corbusier and the Salvation Army built the Cité
de Refuge. Its appearance, some said, resembled a beautiful
ship, "where everything is clean, comfortable, useful, and
gay."[15] But whose discomfort was thereby relieved—the hut
dweller's or everyone else's?

The shack, the shanty, the hut, discomfort us in part because we believe modern huts mean only deprivation and
suffering: the hut equals hovel, and hovels conjure up a
stunted existence: dull, nasty, brutish, and short. Sometimes
this is true, but not always. Social scientists rarely incorpo-
rate "contentment" and "satisfaction" in their surveys, and
anyway, hut dwellers are seldom polled. They do reflect

upon their conditions, however, as this apologia by Guineo—who lives among others on New York's Lower East Side—makes eloquently clear:

> This is something I got to do [with] my life. I figure if I don't do something here, my mind will die. I have to keep doing something here. I am my boss because I know what I have to do, what I need, what I don't need. If I need this, I go to the street anywhere, . . . and I take it over here. I have to do that. I don't know other people, how they do it. I think I gotta do this, I like it. I feel good. It is exercising for me. This is something important, for myself. This is the first time I do something for myself.[16]

Unlike Po-i and Shu-ch'i, Guineo wasn't on the run from political tyranny, but like the desert fathers, his path was uncharted, freely chosen. His house—with its inflatable palm tree, statuary, toy train cars, and clothespin wheel—is both a cabinet of curiosities and a house of little pleasures. But for those who hurry by, with nine-to-five jobs, Guineo and his neighbors are like ornamental hermits, surrogates for a life of essential activity denied by a workaday existence. Like the ornamental hermits of the eighteenth century, to the passerby, Guineo's life provokes contemplation but does not inspire participation.

Still, hurrying by, who among us would not, if only for a moment, envy such an "exercising" experience? Would we not, at least in principle, welcome the chance to do something for ourselves, so our minds will not die? Would anyone not cherish an evening or a weekend in a hut of one's own? For the architect or intern, stuck in a life of thoughtless details, a hut of one's own offers the possibility of carrying a project through to its most thorough, even obsessive solution. It is architecture, perhaps as it first inspired us, though now, in our experience, often lacking a patron for such complete, thoughtful development.

Non-architects, too, can build huts of their own. Here, both expertise and reward are democratic. The person who can drive a nail can, afterwards, decide how well the result pleases. By building one's own hut, a person can have his or her own small, affordable piece of architecture. Even the person lacking land may participate; cities teem with other possibilities.

Living in an apartment one summer gave me a chance to speculate. Outside my window lay a small parapet. Sitting there, I discovered, was not unlike sitting in my backyard hut. Perched against the side of the building, a stream of phenomena no less buoyant than in my backyard caught my attention: car sounds, people sounds, pigeon sounds, smoke in the sky, planes overhead; the stillness of midafternoon, the rush at the end of the day, distant trees in the last sunlight, the air of the city at night, the moon—even the moon.

Yet none of these phenomena existed inside my apartment, except as noise in the high-decibel range. And walking on the street below, my attention was diverted; I was not at home. Had anyone wished, they might have built a very good hut right there on that parapet. I completed several in my mind and also experimented some with what existed there. Bread crumbs attracted sparrows and pigeons. Morning glories could be coaxed out of tin cans and up iron railings. Pans of water caught reflections, and soot. Summer showers plopped against the awning overhead and wetted the edge of the parapet. The rain could have been made to plunk against a more resonant material, and as well, to soak into a dish of moss, or drizzle down an opaque surface, stand in puddles, or even leak inside, staining a wood surface. On my parapet, thirty feet above the city, pure experience was no further away than anyplace else. But even without a parapet or a balcony, the city dweller still has possibilities. Odd bits of structure that have outlived their utility—turrets or elevator housings, for example—suggest sites, either as "found" places or as inspiration for newly built ones.

I explored such a site on a rooftop exactly beneath the superstructure of the Oakland Bay Bridge in San Francisco. As I climbed the stairs to the rooftop, I could already hear the roar of traffic overhead. Sitting there, on a mat behind a screen I had brought to suggest the scale of a potential hut, I

Under the spell of the traffic's subtly changing rhythm
San Francisco, 1988

. . . either as "found" places or inspiration for new
Washington, D.C., 1988

. . . odd bits of former utility—rooftop turrets or elevator housings
Cincinnati, 1989

A city of huts and a city of hut dwellers as well
Washington, D.C., 1988

fell under the spell of the traffic's subtly changing hum. Like a relentlessly flowing mountain stream, this hum recalled to my mind the huts of Chinese and Japanese recluse poets. Here, now, I felt a focus that was perhaps not unlike the source of their inspiration. I could imagine a hut life evolving here, with city sounds ebbing and flowing, night and day, season upon season.

Other sites—the no-man's-land surrounding a housing block, for example—looked foreboding though perversely inviting. What might a row of well-tended huts along its perimeter (a kind of allotment park) do to reclaim such a forlorn landscape?

For me, now, no city remains as I first found it. Each has become a city of huts, and in my imagination, a city of hut dwellers as well. Visiting one another's sites, they climb creaky stairs and slip onto rooftops, balconies, or parapets. There they touch something deep in the needs and memory of people, something that refuses to be dismissed yet is fully alive only in the hut.

Umberto Eco has observed that once we lose our innocence, the expression of basic human emotions must take new forms. The man who loves a sophisticated woman knows he must be careful how he declares his love; his expression must not only avoid false innocence but clearly state that it is no longer easy to speak innocently.[17] He must find a sophisticated container to carry his innocent message.

The contemporary person who wishes to declare a similar emotion about hut life must find a similarly sophisticated container. Clearly, as the Bronx *casitas* have shown, the urge to make such declarations can be so strong as to overcome many obstacles. Still, these places lack sophistication. They speak of a nostalgia peculiar to recent immigrants, which— it is assumed—will pass once the generation who builds them has become fully integrated.

But, "sophisticated containers" exist as much for those who *don't* have memories to fill them as for those who *do*. A sophisticated container juxtaposes past and present: In them, nostalgia and creativity reverberate. Sophisticated containers create *new* memories, even as they invoke old ones.

When I first encountered the tea ceremony, I wondered if this were not the prototype of such a sophisticated container. In its beginning, Tea had been a sophisticated method for refashioning culture. Then, individuals of "low birth" had found their way to positions of national power. By mixing elements of elegant court culture with elements of farm or town life, the early tea men had made a new cultural game out of parts no more disparate than modern life and regional or ethnic identity are today. They found a way to express themselves, as Umberto Eco recommends, in terms worldly and wise. They had repackaged tradition as if for a trip to the big city.

I once used this story to illustrate a larger point—that to gain perspective on life, Tea and activities like it use the world itself in order to abandon the world. I asked my students how much of their lives they spent in what has been called "confections." How much did media-driven experiences divert them from themselves and how much did these divertissements and spectacles cover over the most basic human aspiration—to know what it is to have a human life, as opposed to, say, the life of a dog or a cat.

Then I asked them to imagine an experience that would draw them out of their confectionery world. As they puzzled over my question, a student reframed the task: "You mean, I must use the only world I know—to live the only human life I can be sure I will ever have."

"I couldn't have said it better," I replied. "But now . . . what about it? How will you *do* this?"

Closing Interval

The Hut in the Wasteland

The first hut lay in shambles in California, but its clone endured, whole, in Ohio. During all my hut-gallery experiments, I'd largely forgotten it. But after reinvoking the first hut's magic from only a few of its parts, I now understood that I could revisit that magic again, if I wanted to. I still had the chance.

Crawling inside the Ohio replica, resting among cobwebs, I found myself on eerily familiar ground: tree trunks, though different in kind and placement, still sprung from the ground nearby. And bird cries, though in a different key, still echoed outside. The sun still cast dusty shadows on windows and on the floor, some shadows moving slightly with the breeze the way I remembered.

Even so, the broader context had suffered a radical change. A millennial world now surrounded me—a world of anxiety and hyped values, of jargon-laden talk and failed ideals, a world clinging to remote controls of meaningless choice—"whatever."

Still, in this wasteland of whatever, the hut waited, in no hurry.

But of course, huts have always been supremely at home in the "whatever": in the Buddhists' realm of nonattachment, in the humanists' world of skepticism. Free from aggressively righteous agendas, the wasteland welcomes a contingent community, a *sangha* of silence. In California, we had folded silk triangles into squares, wiping tea containers and scoops; we had let the hut stay empty. In this landscape, the hut posited no answers and posed only the simplest questions.

Here, in Ohio, I would have a new community—wonderfully idiosyncratic, independent souls, each of whom retained a tick or two that differentiated Nanda's tea from Nathan's, Karim's tea from Kat's, Peter's tea from Paul's. Like their *konomi*—the choices they made from among my utensils to compliment those each had made—these differences let each personality emerge out of choreography's uniformity. Like businessmen all dressed in suits, these differences spoke clearly in each face, each gesture, each detail of compliance. They had told me who was who.

Whatever else they might do in life, here in this hut, each of them had accomplished something almost perfect. They had come to know how that felt. Amidst the wasteland's clutter, our hut formed an island of simple pleasure, of "please" and "thank you"—the calm eye in the midst of an ultimately inconsequential storm.

But in the short run, the wasteland—distracted, indifferent—invites anyone intent on setting the world straight. Safe within the circle of architecture and other circles as well, cheery totalitarian optimists promulgate large-scale plans regardless of their small-scale consequences. It seems that every problem must have a solution, all of them blockbusters, and when added together, they foretell a chilly, brave new world. Still, the hut waited and in it, we listened, measuring small-scale consequences and the reality unaffected by them, day by day.

Huts are always fascinating but the huts of sophisticated cultures are especially so: from the huts of ancient recluse poets to those of ornamental hermits, from the *casitas* of the Bronx to the huts of seventeenth-century tea masters, from the shacks of the homeless to the follies of postmodern architects. All these huts deconstruct the optimistic sophistication of their age. Then they rearrange it. Virginia Woolf once advised any woman who wished to write poetry or fiction that nothing was more requisite to her goal than a *room of one's own*. In that room, insulated from masculine sophistication and control, a woman could find her own voice, her own imagination.

Nowadays, the woman—or man—who wishes to *experience* the poetry of life (even before the issue of writing comes up) might be similarly advised to have a hut of her—or his—own. Here, isolated from the wasteland and its new-world saviors, a person might gain perspective on life and the forces that threaten to smother it.

Only in a hut of one's own can a person follow his or her own desires—a rigorous discipline, and one that the poet Gary Snyder calls the hardest of all, presupposing as it does self-knowledge while balancing free action and cultural taboo, knowing whether a desire is instinctive or the imprint of culture, or if personal, whether such desires are the product of thought, of contemplation, or of the unconscious.[18]

Even if this hut is only one's normal abode inhabited in a different way, here in a hut of one's own, a person may find one's very own self, the source of humanity's song.

After reading an early draft of this book, a friend returned it having circled each "we" that he encountered. In the margin he wrote: "Who is the 'we'? Avoid!"

His advice, I realized, was intended to steer me clear of the pretension or false modesty with which authors sometimes evade authorship. By spreading responsibility from "I" to "we," writers can become an amorphous and seemingly irrefutable collective, like the "royal we" of Queen Victoria ("We are not amused."). Unacknowledged, this kind of "we" can leave the reader, like the Queen's subjects, out of the loop. Even so, I realized that my "we" was not evasive but actual; it had formed around a genuine collective that for nearly thirty years—sometimes loosely and sometimes formally—had grounded my thoughts about huts, architecture, and culture.

The "we" of this book, then, began with my master's thesis, *Entertaining the Idea of an American Tea Ceremony, with Special Reference to Its Environment*, at the University of California, in both Berkeley and Davis. The "we" first formed around the advice and encouragement of Joseph Esherick in Architecture, Marian Ury in Japanese and Comparative Literature, and Richard Miller in Japanese History. Shortly after I had written my thesis, other voices joined theirs: a former teacher, Teiji Itoh, added his comments by mail and Kimie Tamura added her instruction in Tea's choreography. To all of these, I owe a great debt. They helped me see not only the potential significance of my work but also its delight.

Still, the idea might have ended then (after I left California for Ohio) were it not for the encouragement I received from Richard Danziger, then president of New York's Urasenke Chanoyu Center, and Lisa Taylor, then director of the Cooper Hewitt Museum. Both were patrons of their own remarkable "American" tearooms, and as Lisa once ob-

Acknowledgments

served, "If you can do it [tea in a hut] in Ohio, then anyone can do it anywhere." But before I had the chance, a timely confluence brought me together with colleagues and students at the Washington/Alexandria Center for Architecture in Virginia. There Jaan Holt, Greg Hunt, Layla Shamash, Chris Pardee, and my Urban Landscape students indulged and expanded my imagination about huts beyond the backyard; together we conjured huts on rooftops, in city plazas, on freeway medians, and in other unlikely places.

Back at Miami University, my Chair, Robert Zwirn, not only encouraged me but, more remarkably, gave his permission to use the rotunda's balcony as my hut's first Ohio site. To John Fabelo I owe that hut's skilled execution and to the next Chair, Robert Benson, I owe the support and encouragement I needed to build my hut-gallery. For that structure's superb execution, I am indebted to Tim Mount and Wenyi Wu. More than craftsmen, John, Tim, and Wenyi were also confidants who mixed together with carpentry tales of growing up and building in Cuba, Ohio, and China. Not only was the "we" growing, it was becoming global.

Helping me think about the relationship between huts and galleries were Dennis Barrie and Jack Sawyer of Cincinnati's Contemporary Arts Center, John Walsh of the J. Paul Getty Museum, and Elizabeth Shepherd at UCLA's Wight Art Museum. At first, we talked about the hut *in* a gallery but later concluded that this would be redundant; the hut already *was*, in and of itself, a gallery. To demonstrate this, I need only use my hut in this way. For the hut-gallery's subsequent exhibitions, I am indebted to the imagination and energy of all the participating artists: Terry Barrett, Seymour Howard, and Gail Della Piana and her students.

Less specific but no less significant were the contributions of others: Mel Weitsman, Meg Gawler Blondel, Hiroko and Junji Tsuzuki, Sonya Schwab, Jacqueline Woodfill, Barbara Carpenter, Lee and Vickie Stewart; Bruce Tully, Dainin and Tomoe Katagiri, Gengo and Yoshie Akiba; Joe Wagner, Tracy Moir, Kaylynn TwoTrees, and Guy Humphrey; Bonnie Mitchell, Kenji Tanaka, Dana Buntrock, and Arnetta Guion; Jack Richards, Tyrone Cashman, Peter Van

Dine, Elizabeth Cahn, Rob Silberman, David Martin, Gini Maddox, William Owsley, Sterling Cook, Susan Ewing, Kirk Swinehart, Hiroko Kiiffner, and Andrew and Mary Rose Schulman. And to all my colleagues and students, I am indebted for their interest and participation—especially Nanda Madi, Nathan Jones, Kathleen Winters, Karim Hammad, Peter Springer, and Paul Lashua.

The decision to move from building to writing owes much to the encouragement I received from those who found interesting the short articles I had already written: Constance Pierce at Miami University, Philip Thiel at the University of Washington, Richard Solomon, then editor of *Inland Architect*, and the editors of *Arcade*. For writing this book, however, I am most indebted to Lee Horvitz. His patience, week after week, hearing me read the first draft made writing a real pleasure and his careful comments, more than once, saved me from my own excesses.

To my other readers I owe a similar debt. More than any other constituency, they formed my sense of the "we." By independently probing my prose for its unintended or misinformed meanings, they let me form my wider sense of authorship: Falken Forshaw, Laurie Van Gelder, Richard Schwab, Lynn Coward, Sergio Sanabria, Linnea Dietrich, Ilya Howard, Bob Hagerty, Agnes Taugner, and Rob Brokob. Other readers provided editorial assistance—Gerald Carpenter and Brian Thomas helped me shape the final manuscript and, for their help, I am very grateful.

Even so, in the final product there will undoubtedly be errors and omissions, and for these, I take sole responsibility.

There from the beginning, seeing me from the first makeshift tatters of the backyard hut to the manuscript's closing interval, and all the steps in between, I owe the greatest debt to Peter Cline. Always the helpful skeptic, I owe whatever rigor I might have achieved at each stage to his loving direction. And for the bridge he helped me build to the generations behind my own, I thank Wayne Rizzo. His dream of huts sustained my own, often providing the inspiration I needed to carry on. In the end, my only regret is that my parents, Mark and Laura Esch, did not live to see the story they helped begin find its way into print. Even so, their lessons about building and living close to nature have been, for me, as profound as they were indelible. And to my aunts and uncle—Esther Kjorstad, Peg Weaver, and John Esch—I extend my thanks for keeping these memories alive.

Still, I have yet to acknowledge those groups upon whose financial generosity my work has depended. Funding for my hut-gallery experiment was made possible by an Ohio Board of Regents Research Challenge Award, while funding for that gallery's exhibitions was made possible by The Graham Foundation for Advanced Study in the Fine Arts. General research support related to this book was provided by The Hampton Fund (for travel in Japan), The Ohio Arts Council Individual Artists Fellowship in Design, the National Endowment for the Humanities Summer Seminar program (specifically Bernd Magnus's seminar in the genealogy of postmodernism), Miami University's Summer Faculty Research Program, and several Architecture Department Travel stipends.

For the year I needed to write this book, I thank my provost, Anne Hopkins, my dean, Hayden May, and my chair, Robert Benson. And for their generous support in allowing the entire year to be productive, I am again indebted to The Graham Foundation. To the School of Fine Arts Development Fund and Special Projects Fund, I owe the support I required to obtain the book's illustrations. Helping me gain permission to use these illustrations were Mika Berkery, Karim Berrada, and Fredrick Courtright; Marcia Olcott and Barbara Wheeler provided valuable clerical and technical assistance. Moreover, working with them all was a pleasure.

Finally, I am grateful to Roger Conover and the MIT Press for supporting this book. As well, I am indebted to Kathleen Caruso for her good judgment and good humor in editing my text and to Jean Wilcox for the book's design. Without their help, the book would not be what it is.

Preface

1. Ann Cline, "Little Houses in the City: An American Tea Ceremony," *Arcade, The Northwest Journal for Architecture and Design* (Seattle, June/July 1990): 8–11.

Chapter One

1. Gaston Bachelard, *The Poetics of Space*, trans. Maria Jolas (1969; reprint, Boston: Beacon Press, 1994), 32.
2. Li Chi, "The Changing Concept of the Recluse in Chinese Literature," *Harvard Journal of Asiatic Studies* 24 (1962–63): 234–247. [The full text of the story is found in Ssu-ma Ch'ien, *Records of the Historian*, Shih chi #61, New York, 1969.]
3. Arthur Waley, *The Way and Its Power: A Study of the Tao Tê Ching and Its Place in Chinese Thought* (New York: Grove Press, 1958), 206.
4. Ibid, 241.
5. Thomas Merton, *The Wisdom of the Desert: Sayings from the Desert Fathers of the Fourth Century* (New York: New Directions, 1960), 6.
6. Ibid., 67–68.
7. Burton Watson, "The Poetry of Reclusion," *Chinese Lyricism: Shih Poetry from the Second to the Twelfth Centuries* (New York: Columbia University Press, 1971), 77, 80–81. The "nourishers of life" refer to seekers of Taoist immortality.
8. Roland Barthes, *The Pleasure of the Text* (New York: Farrar, Strauss and Giroux, 1975), 19.
9. James Agee, *Let Us Now Praise Famous Men* (New York: Houghton Mifflin, 1969), 182.
10. Osvald Siren, *Gardens of China* (New York: Ronald Press, 1949), 5.
11. Po Chu-i, "Planting Bamboos," in *Chinese Poems*, trans. Arthur Waley (1946; reprint, London: Allen & Unwin, 1968), 115.

Notes

12. Edith Sitwell, *English Eccentrics* (Harmondsworth, England: Penguin, 1958), 41.

13. Merton, *Widsom of the Desert*, 5.

14. Marc-Antoine Laugier, *Essai sur L'Architecture* (Paris, 1753), in *On Adam's House in Paradise*, Joseph Rykwert (New York: Museum of Modern Art, 1972), 43–44.

15. Alberto Perez-Gomez, *Architecture and the Crisis of Modern Science* (Cambridge, MA: MIT Press, 1985), 48.

16. Donald Keene, ed. *Anthology of Japanese Literature* (New York: Grove Press, 1955), 197–212.

17. Stephen Toulmin, *Cosmopolis: The Hidden Agenda of Modernity* (Chicago: University of Chicago Press, 1990).

18. Kakuzo Okakura, *The Book of Tea* (New York: Dover, 1964), 30–31.

19. Samuel Taylor Coleridge, "Cristabel," *The Best of Coleridge*, ed. Earl Leslie Griggs (New York: Nelson & Sons, 1934), 64.

20. Dorothy Wordsworth, *The Journals of Dorothy Wordsworth*, ed. Mary Moorman (Oxford: Oxford University Press, 1971), 9.

Chapter Two

1. Francis Bacon, *Gesta Grayorum* (1594), *The Origins of Museums: The Cabinets of Curiosities in Sixteenth- and Seventeenth-Century Europe*, ed. O. R. Impey and A. G. MacGregor, eds. (Oxford/New York: Clarendon Press, Oxford University Press, 1985), 1.

2. Ibid.

3. Michael Foucault, *The Order of Things* (London: Tavistock Publications, 1970), 34.

4. João Rodrigues, *This Island of Japon: João Rodrigues of 16th-Century Japan*, trans. Michael Cooper, S. J. (Tokyo: Kodansha International Ltd., 1973), 264.

5. Ibid., 273.

6. Anthony Vidler, "History of the Folly," in *Follies: Architecture for the Late Twentieth-Century Landscape*, B. J. Archer (New York: Rizzoli, 1983), 10.

7. Diana Ketcham, *Le Desert de Retz: le Jardin Pittoresque de Monsieur de Monville* (San Francisco: Arion Press, 1990), 23.

8. Kurt Schwitters, as quoted in Brian O'Doherty, *Inside the White Cube: The Ideology of the Gallery Space* (San Francisco: Lapis Press, 1986), 43–44.

9. B. J. Archer, *Follies: Architecture for the Late-Twentieth-Century Landscape* (New York: Rizzoli, 1983), 9.

10. M. Saudan and S. Saudan-Skira, *From Folly to Follies* (New York: Abbeville Press, 1987), 103.

11. Jean Starobinski, *L'invention de la Liberté* (Geneva, 1964), as quoted in ibid, 101.

12. Rodrigues, *This Island of Japon*, 278.

13. M. F. K. Fisher, *The Art of Eating* (New York: Vintage, 1976), 252–256.

14. [London] Architectural Association, *Osaka Follies*, 1991, 165.

15. O'Doherty, *Inside the White Cube*, 55.

16. Confucius, IX-28, quoted in Chu'u Chai and Winberg Chai, *Confucianism*, Barron's Educational Series, Inc. (New York: Woodbury, 1973), 39.

17. Robert Farris Thompson, *Flash of the Spirit: African and Afro-American Art and Philosophy* (New York: Random House, 1983), 16.

18. O'Doherty, *Inside the White Cube*, 73, 76.

19. Kakuzo Okakura, *The Book of Tea* (New York: Dover, 1964), 1.

Chapter Three

1. Atsushi Miyatani, "*Pari* Large Tea Meeting," *Shinkenchiku* (October 1993): 221. Translation by Dana Buntrock. The first teahouse is by Tadao Ando, the second by Sai Zaigin.

2. Donald Kuspit, "Depression, Hollywood and Fine Art: The Collapse of Avant Garde Models of Art and the Myth of the Fine Artist," lecture at the Cincinnati Contemporary Arts Center, Cincinnati, 17 September 1994.

3. Ibid.

4. Suzi Gablik, *The Re-enchantment of Art* (New York: Thames and Hudson, 1991), 2.

5. Kuspit, "Depression, Hollywood and Fine Art."

6. Yasuyuki Ogura, "The World of New 'Tea': The Four Principles of *Sabi Eso*," *Shinkenchiku* (November 1993): 225. Translation by Dana Buntrock. The first teahouse is by Kishi Sugimoto, the second and third are by Nakamura and by Tanaka, the fourth is by

Atsushi Kitagawara, and the fifth is by Kisho Kurokawa's younger brother, the architect and product designer Masayuki.

7. Andre Dubus, "A Father's Story," in *The Substance of Things Hoped For*, ed. John B. Breslin (New York: Doubleday, 1988), 152.

8. Anthony Vidler, *The Architectural Uncanny: Essays in the Modern Unhomely* (Cambridge, MA: MIT Press, 1992), 3.

9. Ibid, 4.

10. Bernd Magnus, "The Deification of the Commonplace: *Twilight of the Idols*," in *Reading Nietzsche*, ed. Robert C. Solomon and Kathleen M. Higgins (New York: Oxford University Press, 1988), 167.

11. Jean-François Lyotard, *The Postmodern Condition: A Report on Knowledge*, trans. Geoff Bennington and Brian Massumi (Minneapolis: University of Minnesota Press, 1984), 81.

12. Richard Rorty, *Contingency, Irony and Solidarity* (Cambridge: Cambridge University Press, 1989 [1990]), 44–69.

13. Thomas Fraser Homer-Dixon, "On the Threshold: Environmental Changes as Causes of Acute Conflict," quoted in Robert D. Kaplan, "The Coming Anarchy," *The Atlantic Monthly* (February 1994): 60.

14. Frederick Turner, "The Invented Landscape," in *Beyond Preservation: Restoring and Inventing Landscapes*, ed. A. Dwight Baldwin, Judith de Luce, and Carl Pletsch (Minneapolis: University of Minnesota Press, 1994), 40.

15. Ann Cline, "The Little Hut on the Prairie," in *Beyond Preservation: Restoring and Inventing Landscapes*, ed. A. Dwight Baldwin, Judith de Luce, and Carl Pletsch (Minneapolis: University of Minnesota Press, 1994), 218–219, 224.

16. Jamaica Kincaid, "Homemaking: The Life of a House," *The New Yorker*, 16 October 1995, 62.

17. Gertrude Chandler Warner, *The Boxcar Children* (1942; reprint, Niles, IL: Albert Whitman & Co., 1977), 153–154.

18. Seymour Howard, "Hidden Naos: Duchamp Labyrinths," *Artibus et Historiae* 29 (1994): 168.

19. Ibid, 154.

20. Guy Debord, *Society of the Spectacle* (Detroit: Black & Red, 1983), #1 & 4 [2d printed page].

21. Michael Benedikt, *For an Architecture of Reality* (New York: Lumen Books, 1987), 4.

22. Kenzo Tange, "Tradition and Creation in Japanese Architecture," *Katsura* (New Haven: Yale University Press, 1960), 27.

23. Patrick O'Donovan, "These Blessed Plots of British Freedom," *The Observer* (London), 9 November 1969.

Chapter Four

1. Joseph Rykwert, *On Adam's House in Paradise* (New York: Museum of Modern Art, 1972), 192.
2. Ibid., 14.
3. Gaston Bachelard, *The Poetics of Space*, trans. Maria Jolas (1969; reprint, Boston: Beacon Press, 1994), 33.
4. Ibid.
5. Arthur Schopenhauer, *The World as Will and Representation*, trans. E. F. J. Payne, 2 vols. (1958; reprint, New York: Dover, 1966), 2:391, as quoted in Carl Pletsch, *Young Nietzsche: Becoming a Genius* (New York: The Free Press, 1991), 5.
6. Pletsch, *Young Nietzsche*, 6.
7. Richard Rorty, *Contingency, Irony and Solidarity* (Cambridge: Cambridge University Press, 1989 [1990]), 37.
8. Obituary, *Seattle Times*, 30 January 1996.
9. Robert Venturi, *Complexity and Contradiction in Architecture* (New York: Museum of Modern Architecture/Graham Foundation, 1966), 23.
10. Le Corbusier, *Towards a New Architecture* (1931; reprint, New York: Dover, 1986), 107.
11. Ibid, 227.
12. Herbert Merschamp, "A Crystal Palace of Culture and Commerce," *The New York Times*, 12 January 1997, 45.
13. James Agee, *Let Us Now Praise Famous Men* (1969; reprint, New York: Houghton Mifflin, 1969), 121.
14. Daisetz Suzuki, *Zen and Japanese Culture* (Princeton: Bollingen Series LXIV, 1970), 23, 288.
15. Unsigned article in *Les Temps*, 8 December 1933, as quoted in Brian Brace Taylor, *Le Corbusier: The City of Refuge, Paris, 1929–33* (Chicago: University of Chicago Press, 1987), 111.
16. Diana Balmori and Margaret Morton, *Transitory Gardens, Uprooted Lives* (New Haven: Yale University Press, 1993), 100–103.
17. Umberto Eco, *Postscript to The Name of the Rose* (New York: Harcourt Brace Jovanovich, 1984), 67–68.
18. Gary Snyder, *Earth House Hold* (New York: New Directions Books, 1969), 19.

Frontispiece

© Robert Brockob 1992. Page ii.

one Primitive Huts

1. Courtesy of the Freer Gallery of Art, Smithsonian Institution, Washington, D.C. Page 8.
2. Courtesy of Area Research Center, U. W. La Crosse, Wisconsin. Page 8.
3. Barbara Mildred Jones, *Follies & Grottoes*, Constable, London, 1974. Page 9.
4. Ann Cline. Page 9.
5. Courtesy of the Arthur Ross Foundation, New York. Page 18.
6. Courtesy of Pier Bourgault, St. Jean Port Joli, Quebec. Page 18.
7. Courtesy of Pier Bourgault, St. Jean Port Joli, Quebec. Page 19.
8. Ann Cline. Page 19.
9. C. Arthaud, *Enchanted Visions*, Arthaud/Putnam, 1972. Page 24.
10. Ann Cline. Page 24.
11. C. Arthaud, *Enchanted Visions*, Arthaud/Putnam, 1972. Page 25.
12. Courtesy of the National Household Museum, Nara. Page 25.
13. Ann Cline. Page 30.
14. Ann Cline. Page 31.
15. Ann Cline. Page 34.
16. Ann Cline. Page 35.

two Experimental Lives

1. Courtesy of Art Resource, New York. Page 40.
2. Yabunouchi Ennan, Courtesy of the Yabunouchi Foundation. Page 40.

Illustration Credits

3. Courtesy of The Litho Shop, Inc./The Lapis Press, Inc., Venice, CA. Page 41.
4. Courtesy of Rodolfo Machado/Jorge Silvetti, Boston. Page 41.
5. Courtesy of Michel Saudan, Geneva. Page 48.
6. Courtesy of Architekturbüro Bolles-Wilson, Munster. Page 48.
7. Courtesy of the Dukes County Historical Society, Edgartown, Massachusetts. Page 49.
8. Standard Oil of New Jersey Collection, courtesy of Photo Archives, Ekstrom Library, University of Louisville. Page 49.
9. Courtesy of Birney Imes, *Juke Joint*, University Press of Mississippi, 1990. Page 58.
10. Courtesy of Takeshi Nishikawa, Kyoto. Page 58.
11. Robert W. Rydel, *World's Fairs: The Century of Progress Expositions*, University of Chicago Press, 1993, Nederlands Foto and Grafisch Centrum. Page 59.
12. Ann Cline. Page 59.
13. Guy Humphrey. Page 64.
14. Guy Humphrey. Page 64.
15. Guy Humphrey. Page 66.

three Ritual Intentions

1. Courtesy of Atsushi Miyatani, A. D. A. Architects and Planners, Paris. Page 72.
2. Courtesy of Kitano-Tenman-gu, Kyoto. Page 72.
3. Courtesy of Outline, New York. Page 73.
4. Courtesy of Takeshi Nishikawa, Kyoto. Page 73.
5. Courtesy of Taian-Myokian, Kyoto. Page 80.
6. Ann Cline. Page 80.
7. Courtesy of L. A. Louver, Venice, California. Page 85.
8. Courtesy of The Bernice P. Bishop Museum, Honolulu. Page 90.
9. Courtesy of Albert Whitman & Co, Morton Grove, Illinois © 1942, 1950, 1969, 1977. Page 90.

Index

Recluses, 3–8, 10–14, 22, 32, 33, 45, 57, 95, 96, 128, 131
Ressentiment, 119
Rikyu, Sen no, 78, 79, 84
Rinkan chanoyu, 47
The Road Warrior, 82
Robertson, Jack, 44
Robinson Crusoe, 92
Rodrigues, João, 39, 42
Rorty, Richard, 84, 114
Rosenblatt, Roger, 94
Rousseau, Jean Jacques, 13, 22, 23, 60
Russian formalists, 46
Rykwert, Joseph, 112

Sacramento Valley (Calif.), 33
St. Anthony, 3
Saloon/salon, 99
Sangha, 130
Santa Maria del Fiore, 115
Sakui, 84
San Juan, 21
Seaside (Fla.), 61
Seiza, 77
Schnabel, Julian, 75
Schwitters, Kurt, 43, 44
Shimenawa, 118
Shinto, 118
Shin-yin, 10
Shuko, Murata, 23, 26, 27, 29, 39, 47
Sitio, 29
Silver Pavilion, 26
Sitwell, Dame Edith, 12
Six Degrees of Separation, 54
Smoke, 117
Snyder, Gary, 132
The Sound of Music, 82
Spyri, Johanna, 3
Sue (in *How to Cook a Wolf*), 50, 51, 96